B P KOIRALA
LIFE AND TIMES

B P KOIRALA
LIFE AND TIMES

KIRAN MISHRA

WISHWA PRAKASHAN
(A Division of Wiley Eastern Limited)
NEW DELHI • BANGALORE • BOMBAY • CALCUTTA
GUWAHATI • HYDERABAD • LUCKNOW • MADRAS • PUNE

WISHWA PRAKASHAN
(A Division of Wiley Eastern Limited)

NEW DELHI	:	4835/24, Ansari Road, Daryaganj, New Delhi 110 002
BANGALORE	:	27, Bull Temple Road, Basavangudi, Bangalore 550 004
BOMBAY	:	Saraswati Mandir School, Nana Chowk, Kennedy Bridge, Bombay 400 007
CALCUTTA	:	40/8, Ballygunge, Circular Road, Calcutta 700 019
GUWAHATI	:	Pan Bazar, Rani Bari, Guwahati 781 001
HYDERABAD	:	1-2-412/9, Gaganmahal, Near A.V. College, Domalguda, Hyderabad 500 029
LUCKNOW	:	18, Madan Mohan Malviya Marg, Lucknow 226 001
MADRAS	:	No. 6, 1st Main Road, Gandhi Nagar, Madras 600 020
PUNE	:	Indira Cooperative Housing Society Ltd., Indira Heights, Flat No. 2, Building No. 7, Erandawane, Karve Road, Pune 411 038

ISBN : 81-7328-022-3

Published by V.S. Johri for Wishwa Prakashan
(A Division of Wiley Eastern Limited)
4835/24, Ansari Road, Daryaganj, New Delhi 110 002; and
Composed by : Spectrum Media, New Delhi 110 002
and printed by : Ram Printograph, New Delhi.

PRINTED IN INDIA

Dedicated to
Shri Jaya Mani Dixit
Rani Rebati Debi

PREFACE

Ever since I translated and published B.P. Koirala's novel *Narendra Dai* into Hindi in 1985, it has been my fond dream to look into the life of that man. The present book is a realisation of that dream in some way. BP, a humanist, socialist, who remained committed to his principles and beliefs through to the end of his life, had also aim of bringing the King of Nepal out of his royal palace to common people's homes.

Born in an ordinary Nepali middle class family, BP rose to international fame by his humanism, his magnanimity, outstanding leadership, political achievements and above all international outlook. He had a multi-faceted personality. A believer in Gandhian philosophy and method of non-violence in the struggle for human liberation, he was influenced by Marx's dialectics and historical materialism. Not in the least he was a poet in prose, a romantic who touched the heart of millions. Yet he was revolutionary who successfully led the Nepali Congress Party in an armed struggle against Rana Regime. His contribution to the establishment of democracy in Nepal in 1950s and again as an inspiring beacon in its recent restoration, notwithstanding the dark period from 1960s to 1980s, remains incomparable. He had his failings too, as no man is given to roses all the way.

It is difficult, if not impossible to comprehend such a personality. In the present book I have tried to capture the diversity and richness of BP's personality. However, it is left to the reader to judge how far this attempt has been successful. The material for the book has been gathered from diverse sources. Among published sources BP's own political and literary writings, articles, interviews, specially late Bhola Chatterji's *conversations* with BP, a life-long friend of BP, have been used extensively. Material obtained through personal interviews with BP's associates, contemporaries and family members have been very rewarding. In particular, I am extremely grateful to Prime Minister, Girja Prasad Koirala who took out time for me, shared his remembrances of his brother over cups of tea and answered whatever questions I put to him. Shailendra Kumar Upadhyay, a former Communist leader who among others had founded the Nepal Communist Party and had been foreign minister under the King's regime extensively shared his views with me. Govind Prasad Upadhyay, the famous leader of the Nepal Prajaparishad not only obliged me with an interview but flooded me with documents and literature relating to the Prajaparishad. I managed to motivate Iswari Raj Misra, an ex-justice of Nepal to give me access to his memoirs he has been writing. I wish to convey my deep sense of gratitude to all of them. BP's family members and relatives viewed my work with sympathy and readily offered all possible help. The most enriching experience was the interview with BP's wife, Shushila Koirala. Her serene face and sensitive eye immediately established a rapport, a communion. These interviews would not have been possible without financial support from the Indo-Nepal B.P. Koirala Foundation. For this I am particularly indebted to Professor Bimal Prasad, India's Ambassador to Nepal and His Excellency Chakra P. Bastola in New Delhi.

The manuscript of the work was read by several friends and colleagues. Professor Anirudha Gupta who has published several books on Nepal's political affairs benefitted me with his comments and helpful suggestions. Professor Devendra Bhusan Gupta, Dr. Suren Navlakha, Dr. D.N. Dwivedi and Kamalesh Sukla deserve my gratitude for reading through the manuscript at various stages of its development.

I am grateful to C.M.P. Sivadasan of the Institute of Economic Growth library for his constant support by making available published literature of relevance. Sher Singh Bisht typed the manuscript. To him, to Stella Saleth, K. Lal, Raman Raj Mishra and V.S. Johri. I simply say, *Thank You*. Finally, my own little group of seven has been a source of strength. When the manuscript started taking shape, Amitabh, Charudutt and Kumar felt that "good times seem to have really returned", and that inspired me to complete the work.

KIRAN MISHRA

CONTENTS

CONTENTS

1

FAMILY AND EARLY LIFE

September 8, 1914 was a memorable day in the life of Dibyadevi. On that day in the ancient and holy city of Kashi, on the banks of river Ganges, she gave birth to her first son Bisheswar Prasad Koirala. Dibyadevi was the second wife of Krishna Prasad Koirala. She had come to Kashi from Biratnagar to take care of her aged mother-in-law who had opted, following a Hindu belief,[1] to live in Kashi for the rest of her life. Performing the ritual of *Kashivas* in the last phase of one's life was a luxury those days which only the rich could afford. Krishna Prasad Koirala could afford it for his mother. He had established a sound business in Nepal Tarai. The youngest son of Nandikeshwar Upadhyaya (who died quite young) Krishna Prasad grew to be a self-made man.

From his ancestral home in Dumja, a village 36 kilometres east of Kathmandu, Krishna Prasad had migrated to Biratnagar, then a small hamlet in the south-east of Kathmandu.

Soon after settling there, he got a Kali temple built and then plunged into business, acquired large property and developed a network of business establishments. Knowledgeable people relate that it was Krishna Prasad who had converted, the hamlet Biratnagar, into a commercial and industrial centre. Later he had become Custom Collector of the whole Tarai belt. In those days, this post was auctioned to the highest bidder of Nepal. Later on, he had also become the sole agent for imported cigarettes in Nepal from Darjeeling across the Indo-Nepal border.

Those were the days when prosperous Nepali citizens used to journey to Calcutta and Kashi, but for different reasons. Calcutta provided exclusive tailoring, shoes made to order, best landau to ride, pleasure houses, theatre and a haven for the 'dandies'. To Kashi, it was a religious call, a dip in the holy Ganges, ride on an *ekka* or a tonga and Banarasi *mithai, puri* and *kachauri* to eat.

These cities held also fond memories for Nepali rebels against the ruling Ranas, who used to escape to India and take shelter in these cities during the late nineteenth century.

FATHER : A SOCIAL REFORMER

Krishna Prasad had every reason to be proud of his achievements. He had two wives, a flourishing business, nine children, and more wealth than a Brahmin could ever dream of. He was a father of six sons — Matrika Prasad being the eldest, then Bisheswar Prasad, Keshab Prasad, Tarini Prasad and Girja Prasad. In between these was another son who died in infancy. He had four daughters — Nalini, Indira, Soubhagya and Vijayalaxmi.

Once, while going on a business trip on his horse, he introspected on his own life and achievements.

He had done everything for his family, but he wondered, what had he done for his less fortunate countrymen? The thought kept haunting him for long until he announced to his family and friends that he wanted to construct a hospital and a school in Biratnagar. Many well-wishers tried to disuade him on the ground that it was an exclusive sphere of the state and if he went on this mission, the Ranas would certainly take umbrage at this sort of defiance to their authority. It would certainly have been unwise to incur the displeasure of the ruling Ranas.

Nepal under Prime Ministership of Shri Chandra Shamsher Jung Bahadur Rana was not a congenial place for any sort of civic activism. Reformist movements, like the one initiated by Shri Madhav Raj Joshi on the lines of Arya Samaj, were crushed in no time. Joshi himself was caned in public and put behind the bars. The Ranas and the priestly Brahmins had all connived to suppress any reformist movement in Nepal. But these movements, howsoever small or ephemeral, had lasting effect on the minds of the common people. It would not be out of place to mention an episode to which I was a witness as a child. My father, who belonged to a rich Brahmin family with close proximity to the Rana ruling class, was sent to India by the then Prime Minister of Nepal to take care of a Rana lady married to a Raja of a small estate in the United Provinces (now Uttar Pradesh). As the lady lost her husband shortly after her marriage, my father had to stay back in India to manage her estate. With his status, it was a matter of prestige in those days that we were sent to an English medium convent school in India. One summer vacation, my father took us to Kathmandu and the whole family went to pay respects to Prime Minister, Mohan Shamsher. As soon as we were given audience, the PM said to my father, pointing towards me, being the eldest among the girls, "Jaya, I am told that you want your children to become Christian; you are sending them to a Christian missionary school." My father, who had early in life learnt the ways of his ruler, promptly replied, "Sarkar, I am sending them to the best school in India with the hope that once trained, they will come and serve my masters to the best of their abilities." The Rana nodded affirmatively. Thus was ensured our educational future. Only those families which were in close proximity with the Ranas could give English education to their children. All other citizens had to follow their traditional vocations for earning their livelihood. Any deviation from the prescribed norms provoked immediate retaliation from the Ranas.

In spite of repressive social conditions and despotic Rana rule, Krishna Prasad Koirala went ahead with his plans. He went to Calcutta, looking for a teacher for his school and a doctor for the hospital in Biratnagar. The two-some who came with him eventually became his friends and helped Krishna Prasad Koirala to renounce wordly pursuits for a higher goal in life. He had also started writing in Nepali on the political affairs of the country. Besides, he set up a women's organization in Biratnagar. His wife and sister became, respectively, its President and Secretary. At his initiative, a letter was sent to the Prime Minister's wife in Kathmandu requesting her to become the patron of this organisation. Naturally, the request was ignored.

All that Krishna Prasad was doing, other than his business, was not to the liking of the Ranas. As it seems, he was destined to incur the wrath of the Prime Minister. It so happened that on one winter morning in the early 1920, Krishna Prasad Koirala saw a man on his way to India in search of a job. It was a bitterly cold morning and, in that biting cold, the haggard had only tattered clothes on him which could scarcely cover his body. Krishna Prasad was badly moved by the miserable condition of the man. The first thing he did was that he gave that man new clothes to wear and took his tattered ones. When he reached home, he requested his wife to make a parcel of the rags. He sent that parcel to the Prime Minister of Nepal, along with a letter. The letter stated, "I am afraid, when the parcel is opened, it may create some consternation in the Durbar. But I want Your Highness to understand the conditions in which your subjects live." BP who narrated this episode in the seventies in an interview observed that his father "was a social reformer and not a rebel in the beginning. He just wanted the Government to be aware of the miserable economic conditions of the people. It was farthest from his mind to go against the Government. [But] Circumstances willed otherwise and forced him to act in a manner which he would have willingly avoided."[2]

FAMILY IN EXILE

This incident could not go without invoking punishment. A warrant of arrest for the whole family was issued from Kathmandu. The Bada Hakim (Collector of the district) who was a friend, helped Krishna Prasad and his family to sneak into India, by delaying the execution of the warrant. This was the beginning of Koirala family diaspora— forty-five persons belonging to five families, dependent on Krishna Prasad for their living had to flee the country. They somehow managed to reach Banaras. Their properties in Biratnagar and Kathmandu were attached by Rana Government. Krishna Prasad became a pauper overnight. At the age of thirty-five, the head of a very large family was on the verge of beggary. He went around in search of food and shelter. No wonder, people who knew Krishna Prasad well, called him the *Mahatma of Nepal*. Krishna

Prasad was not a man to worry and brood about the future. He was a man of action, devoted to his cause. He was a sensitive man. Nobody had asked him to leave his comfortable hearth and home, to plunge into poverty, and take up the cause of the downtrodden.

While in Banaras, Krishna Prasad joined the Indian National Congress and took active part in India's freedom movement. It was his considered belief that there would be no liberation for the people of Nepal from the yoke of the Ranas unless India achieved her independence. During the early decades of the 20th century, this had become a matter of conviction of Nepalese intelligentsia that unless India attained freedom, there was no question of ending the centuries-old Rana autocracy in Nepal. The extent of Krishna Prasad's involvement with Indian cause can be seen from the fact that whatever foreign clothes the Koiralas had brought from Biratnagar were consigned to flames on Gandhi's call during the Swadeshi movement. A Calcutta 'dandy', Krishna Prasad Koirala now became a Khadi clad social worker. After a few months of their stay in Banaras, it became clear that they could not afford to live there and support the whole retinue of dependents. Some friends from Bihar had offered to help. So the family packed off for Saharsa. In a way, it was good since Saharsa was closer to Nepal. But the place they were provided with was near the Kosi which flooded for almost three months in a year. People had to seek shelter on tree-tops, *machans* and boats. To add to the miseries of the Koirala family, Kosi changed its course in one rainy season to over-run the village, compelling them to return to Banaras.

KRISHNA PRASAD JOINS INDIAN FREEDOM MOVEMENT

Those were the days when freedom movement in India under the leadership of Mahatma Gandhi had acquired considerable momentum. Gandhiji had given it a direction and taken to Charkha as a symbol of economic and political liberation. The Indian National Congress Working Committee had issued the Purna Swaraj day resolution (Jan. 26, 1930) for adoption at public meetings all over India. The resolution, inter alia, said, "village industries, such as hand spinning, have been destroyed, leaving the peasantry idle for at least four months in the year, and dulling their intellect for want of handicrafts and nothing has been substituted, as in other countries, for the craft thus destroyed.[3] It was against this background that the call for boycott of foreign clothes and for adoption of Khadi was given. BP recalls : "I think ours was one of the few families in Banaras that took to Khaddar in the early 1930." Dibyadevi used to go and spin at Gandhi ashram which brought some money to the family kitty.

BP STEPS IN POLITICS

While Krishna Prasad was actively participating in India's freedom struggle, his son, Bisheshwar Prasad, stepped in political arena on his own, at a very young age.

Influenced by the political atmosphere of the early thirties and Mahatma Gandhi's call for civil disobedience movement, BP stood up in his class at the school in Banaras and said, "I leave my school." With these words a social revolutionary was born.

Remembering his elder brother, Prime Minister Girja Prasad recalled in an exclusive interview, "we lost our father when I was quite young. BP was a father figure to me. He gave me political training. As a young boy, I used to love listening to his exploits as Congress socialist party worker." Indian National Congress wanted only those who believed in non-violence to join the freedom movement. The resolution passed on   September 28th, 1929 in Lucknow relating to Civil Disobedience movement by the All India Congress Committee ran: "In the opinion of the Working Committee, civil disobedience should be initiated and controlled by those who believe in non-violence for purpose of achieving Purna Swaraj, as an article of faith, and as Congress contains in its organization not merely such men and women but also those who accept non-violence as a policy essential in existing circumstances in the country, the Working Committee welcomes the proposal of Mahatma Gandhi and authorises him and those working with him who believe in non-violence as an article of faith to the extent indicated above to start civil disobedience as and when they desire and in a manner and to the extent they decide."[4]

At a time when non-violent civil disobedience movement was gradually gaining strength, a section of youth, which was not satisfied by its slow pace, took to violent methods for quicker attainment of the swaraj. Many young men were drawn to the terrorist movement in 1932. Karachi Congress was held under a gloom cast by the news of the execution of Bhagat Singh, Raj Guru and Sukh Dev. They went to the gallows singing patriotic songs.

At that time, Bisheswar Prasad, a student of Class IX had associated himself with those who had taken arms to over-throw the British rule. His involvement with a terrorist group landed him and his elder brother, Matrika Prasad Koirala, in jail. Koirala brothers were arrested as suspects in 'Moulania Case'. This case was named after a big robbery and murder committed by a gang in Bettiah district of Bihar. The leader of the gang Chandraman Shukla, was hanged and another member Yogendra Shukla got transportation for life in the Andamans. So was Basawan Singh who, after India's independence, became well known trade unionist and a leader of the Socialist Party. After three months in jail, they were set free since the witnesses failed to identify them at the identification parade. It was sheer luck which got them off so easily. It was a close brush with death or life-long transportation.

On Gandhiji's call for Civil Disobedience Movement, jails in the United Provinces (now Uttar Pradesh), Bihar and Gujarat had started filling up with Satyagrahis. For the first time men, women and children belonging to all walks of life started facing policemen's battons and went to jail without any hesitation. BP was again arrested for taking active part in the Jute Mill Worker's Strike in Darbhanga, Bihar.

After his release from jail, BP returned to his studies. Now onwards, he took his studies seriously though he shuttled between Banaras and Calcutta quite often. He was sent to Calcutta because Krishna Prasad thought that Banaras was a village compared to Calcutta. BP, however, was more comfort-able in Banaras than in any other city of India. This was a place of his own choice, though later it was Patna in Bihar which had become close to his heart. The bondage with the Ganges and Banaras acquired early in childhood remained strong all through his life. "Banaras", he would say, "is my second home."

BP earned his Bachelor's Degree from the Banaras Hindu University in 1935 and his Law degree in 1937 from Calcutta. He never appeared for the Master's degree. His father wanted him to practise law. His elder brother, Matrika Prasad Koirala, who had become a Government servant in Nepal, wanted him to join his Majesty's service. BP hesitated for he could not feel free in Nepal during that oppressive period of its history. Matrika Babu was angry. He thought, says BP, "I was a waster". His complaint was, "I was spurning a fortune like that while he had to work hard to earn for the family."

FAMILY RETURNS TO NEPAL

After the death of Prime Minister Chandra Shamsher Jung Bahadur Rana in 1929, Krishna Prasad and his family were allowed to return to Nepal. After he came back, Krishna Prasad bought some land in Biratnagar and plunged into social work. In 1939, he opened cells at different places in Nepal to provide shelter to the political refugees who escaped from India. This naturally angered the British Government. Nepalese authorities promptly took action against him to please the British. In 1942, Krishna Prasad was arrested in Biratnagar and his son (BP) was arrested in Patna. A few months after his arrest, Krishna Prasad was taken to Kathmandu jail. The condition of Nepalese jails under the Ranas was so bad that few could survive.[5] Krishna Prasad died in jail at the age of 57, a day before his illustrious son, Bisheswar Prasad was released from the Indian jail.

So ended the life of a pioneer of social and political cause in Nepal. His body was taken from jail to Arya Ghat for cremation. Dibyadevi not only witnessed the death of her husband but also later faced a similar situation, when her son struggled between life and death in the same Rana prison. Only a lady with iron will could have controlled herself and she did behove a wife of a great man.

Krishna Prasad must have gone through many happy moments of life, thinking that his son would make a place for himself in the struggle for freedom from the Ranas. He knew that his dreams of a democratic Nepal would be achieved by his son while he himself saw his own death coming.

REFERENCES

1. Those who die in Kashi get *Moksha* (salvation).
2. *Portrait of a Revolutionary: BP Koirala* by Bhola Chatterji, Ankur Publishing House, Delhi, p. 63.
3. *The History of Indian National Congress*, Vol. 1, 1885-1935, Pattabhi Sitaramayya, Padma Publications Ltd., Bombay, p. 368.
4. *The History of Indian National Congress*, Vol. 1, p. 369.
5. Describing the conditions in Nepali jails during those days *Nepal Today* commented in its editorial, "Political prisoners whom the Nepali Government regard as sworn foes are treated worst than criminals; they are handcuffed, fettered and chained, ring leaders being neckcuffed with hanging iron balls weighing three to five seers. And they are kept in segregation in narrow cells called *goalghars* which reminded one of Black Hole of Calcutta." *Nepal Today*, July 1950, Vol. II.

2

POLITICAL APPRENTICESHIP AND PARTICIPATION IN INDIA'S FREEDOM STRUGGLE

BP had acquired an awareness of econo-political problems of the society and the nation from his father. He enriched his inheritance with his own experience and understanding. For some time, however, he had not joined any party or political group. He remained a self-styled political worker for student community. His initiation into party politics was a matter of accident. He was once sent by his father to look for a business opening in Bombay. While he was returning, after completing his mission, he met the members of the Communist Party of India at Bombay, V.T. on their way to Meerut. These included Shripad Amrit Dange. This opened a new horizon for him. Back in Banaras he started attending Marxist study circles and reading Communist literature. Every evening he would go to the Engineering College in the Banaras Hindu University to listen to Radio Moscow. Belonging to a group devoted to one aim, living in a commune, debating on Party's directives and discussing international issues was a new experience.

Russian Revolution of October 1917 was looked upon by the Indian revolutionaries as a triumph of the hungry masses over Czarist autocracy. This gave hope for the Indian masses to fight for independence and socialism. The Communist uprising in China under the leadership of Mao-Tsetung was followed closely.

BP developed into a serious dialectician. He had accepted only part of Marxist dialectics. He said, "I am a Marxist in the sense that I have accepted the Marxist methodology in enumerating how a society evolves." But for BP that was only one part of the issue. In his own opinion, "each individual has his own perceptions and had to find his own path to happiness. A happy man had to be true to himself and at peace. Happiness too had many faces."

He further observed, "I was on probation in the Communist Party but my progress was very tardy. I was not very happy in that company for two or three reasons; one of which was that my natural sympathies were with Trotsky who I thought was more of an internationalist than Stalin who was a nationalist. The manner in which Stalin dealt with Trotsky was very distasteful to me."

Sailendra Kumar Upadhyaya, the ex-Foreign Minister of Nepal and ex-member of the Communist Party, recalls, "I don't claim to have known BP well as I was a communist and he a social democrat. It was he who was the first one to have put doubts in my mind about the success of communism."

A sensitive man, BP could not appreciate the doctrinaire attitude which the Communist Party took towards the liberation movement in India. The Sixth World Congress of the Communist International passed a resolution on the 1st Sept. 1928, under the heading *Communist Strategy and Tactics*, which inter alia said, "The Communists must unmask the national reformism of the Indian National Congress and oppose all the phases of the Swarajists, Gandhists etc. about passive resistance."[1]

BP who had all along identified himself with the Indian National Congress and Mahatma Gandhi, found this resolution too harsh : "I had matriculated from my blind adoration of Gandhism. I still retain great admiration for Gandhi and his movement. Their's, that is the Communist's, vulgar criticism of Gandhi's national movement and Gandhi as a person was anathema to me." Although BP had started the nucleus of a Communist Students Organisation and was its Secretary, he was kept on probation for long. He was never upgraded from this level for he had many doubts in his mind and such an attitude, had no place in the party.

A new phase of his political career began in 1934 when BP came in contact with the Indian socialists. He started discussing his reservations about Communism and the Indian Communist movement with Jai Prakash Narayan, popularly called 'JP'. JP himself, a member of the Communist Party of the USA, was not happy with what had happened in the Soviet Union. BP was very happy in JP's company. He says, "I felt I had found the man I could work under." They shared their doubts. JP would try to clarify the doubts of this young man to the best of his ability. JP helped BP as much as he could to clarify objectively the moral dilemma involved in the Communist doctrinarie approach to human problems. Meanwhile the Socialist Party was formed and a foundation conference was held in Patna. "These disillusioned Congressmen of Socialist persuasion organised groups, first in the provinces of Bihar in 1931. Later in Nasik central prison (1932-33) then in the provinces of Bombay and the United Provinces (1933-34). This group collectively constituted the initiating hard core of Congress Socialist Party. Ten of these persons constituted the heart of leadership."[2] These young socialists were each influenced by Marxism, social democracy, and democratic socialism. They endeavoured to combine Marxism and class struggle with the Gandhian concept of decentralization, and the use of non-violent civil disobedience techniques for nationalist and class struggle.

By now BP had identified himself with socialism. The formation of the socialist group within Congress showed him the way to his future political activities. It would be interesting, in this regard, to look back at this phase of the Indian National Movement. Civil disobedience movement had generated great political awareness in the minds of the Indian people. Young leaders of the Congress Party like Sampurnanand, Keshav Dev Malviya, Acharya Narendra Dev, Rafi Ahmed Kidwai, Acharya Kripalani, were trying to find ways and means of developing closer ties with the Indian masses by actively participating in their day-to-day life and struggle for existence. Gandhiji in the midst of such hectic activities, suddenly gave a call for the termination of the Civil Disobedience Movement on the ground that "masses have not received the full message of Satyagraha owing to its adulteration in the process of transmission. It became clear to me that spiritual instruments suffer in their potency when their use is taught through non-spiritual media."[3]

The termination of Civil Disobedience Movement was seen by the younger members of the party as a grievous loss of opportunity. They felt cheated. In this chaos, All India Congress Committee met in Patna. It was here that these young leaders decided to form the Congress Socialist Party. Jai Prakash Narayan was given the responsibility of preparing the draft constitution. Gandhiji, on hearing about the formation of the new party in Wardha, said, "I have welcomed the formation of the Socialist group. Many of these are respected and self-sacrificing workers."[4]

It was hoped that the Congress Socialist Party would press for the adoption of more militant tactics in the nationalist and anti-colonial struggle and play more progressive role in bringing about social and economic reforms in the country. One feels that having groped in the dark for long, BP got the idea about the path he would adopt in the years to come and started working on those lines.

In collaboration of his friends, Narayan Rajeswar Prasad, younger brother of Jai Prakash Narayan, Devendra Prasad Singh, Mahaveer Prasad Sinha, L.K. Jha, Rajeswar Rao and Deva Kanta Borooah, BP formed a study circle[5] in Banaras Hindu University. The bond established between the comrades of this study circle remained strong all through their lives. On an invitation from one of his friends, BP had moved to Darjeeling for a year in 1938, where he had, at one time, thought of practising law. But, this was not to be. When the World War II broke out, he thought of returning to Patna and work for the Congress Socialist party. He was however facing the problem of supporting his family. Devendra Prasad Singh, who later became a lawyer at Patna High Court, had a tacit understanding with him that he would take care of his family, so that BP could whole-heartedly devote his time to politics. This undertaking made him a free man. He became very active in the Socialist movement. His socialist activities landed him in jail several times during the war years of 1939-41, "but not for very long."[6]

The atrocities perpetrated by the Ranas on the political activist was much tyrannical than those by the colonial power in India. About the British rule in India, BP observed later, "You have to understand that Gandhi's movement was possible only under British rule. No other dictatorial authority could have permitted Gandhi to exist... It was not a good model for democracy, this British system in India. But still we could compare what obtained in our country with what obtained in India. So we found that it was easier to live in India than in our country. Whenever we came out of Nepal to India we found ourselves in a freer climate. We could speak our mind, we could even say that British rule was bad, we could get Indian newspapers criticising the British in no uncertain terms. So that was the training I received when I was a student, both in school and when I worked in the national revolutionary movement in India. I got my political training and my democratic philosophy from my participation in the Indian National Struggle, and from my membership of the Socialist Party of India". This was not possible in Nepal.

BP's ideological goal was to establish 'democratic socialist society' as a synthesis of realism, Gandhism and Marxism, which was also the cherished goal of Congress Socialist Party of India from its very inception. He worked for two years as the secretary of Congress Socialist Party. At times he was sent to organise and bring unity among the student movement all over India. During the war years he was thrice arrested in Bihar. He was again arrested for participating in the 1942 Quit India Movement and remained in jail for almost two and half years.

In 1942, Gandhi's Quit India slogan led to the arrest of almost all the national leaders. BP was kept for six months in Bankipur jail where Dr. Rajendra Prasad too was imprisoned. He was shifted later to Hazaribagh Jail and there he met Jagjivan Ram.

After the arrest of front rank leaders of the Quit India Movement, Dr. Ram Manohar Lohia took charge of the "underground All India Congress Committee". He started organising resistance movement against the British. Jai Prakash Narayan, after his sensational escape from Hazaribagh Jail, joined Lohia in his hideout in Nepal. Their effort was short-lived, as they were arrested by the Rana Police and lodged in a jail in Saptari in Nepal.

The people of Saptari broke open the Hanuman Nagar Jail where these revolutionary Socialist leaders were externed and set them free. As a result of this act of defiance, a reign of terror was let loose in that district and some 22 arrests were made by the Rana police.[7] BP was at that time working clandestinely among the British Gurkha soldiers in Dehradun persuading them to defy the British orders of suppressing the nationalist movement. He was arrested and deported to central jail in Hazaribagh in 1942. This sojourn in the jail lasted for about three years.

It may be mentioned here that it was in Hazaribagh jail that BP developed the throat trouble which lasted till the end of his life. Thinking that he was suffering from spurted tonsillitis, the jail doctors sent him to Ranchi hospital under military escort where an operation was performed. The operation did not help much. The doctors who examined him in Patna after his release from the jail could not diagnose his illness. Meanwhile, the All India Congress Committee decided to hold its conference in Bombay on 8th July 1946. On Dr. Rajendra Prasad's insistence, BP went to Bombay where Dr. Duggan, Director of the Tata Cancer Research Institute, diagnosed BP's ailment as throat cancer. This was a blow to Rajen Babu — he was greatly upset. For the next six months BP stayed in the hospital for his treatment.

REFERENCES

1. M.N. Roy too was similarly disillusioned by the Communists on the issue of 'Man' he said, "man did not emerge from the process of evolution with a hammer in his hand but with a distinctive brain". M.N. Roy, *The Twenty Two Thesis of Radical Democracy*. Both BP and M.N. Roy were great humanists.
2. The ten leaders were Jai Prakash Narayan, Ram Manohar Lohia, Ashok Mehta, Acharya Narendra Dev, Achyut Patwardhan, M.R. Masani, Kamladevi, Purshottam Tricumdas, Yusuf Meherally and Ganga Sharan Sinha. (*Leadership and Political Institutions in India*, Richard L. Park and Irene Tinker, Princeton, 1969, p. 189).
3. *The History of Indian National Congress*, Dr. Pattabhi Sitaramayya, Vol. I, p. 569.
4. *The History of Indian National Congress*, Vol. I, 1985-1935, p. 58.
   Jai Prakash Narayan during those days was repeatedly telling his

followers, "We are placing before the Congress a programme and we want the Congress to accept it. If the Congress does not accept it we do not say we are going out of the Congress. If today we fail tomorrow we will try and if tomorrow we fail we will try again", *Indian Struggle for Independence*, Bipan Chandra, p. 305, Viking.

Jai Prakash Narayan observes in his book *Why Socialism?* Today more than ever before it is possible to say that there is only one type, one theory of Socialism-Marxism. Several other groups had developed on the left lines during 1930s, M.N. Roy had organised a strong group of Royists, in 1939. Hindustan Socialist Republican Association, the Revolutionary Socialist Party and Various Trotskyist groups also functioned in 1930.

5. Many of the present-day Indian leaders like Madhu Dandvate, Madhu Limaye, Surendra Mohan and even Chandra Shekhar as young students used to attend this study circle.

6. *Portrait of a Revolutionary : B.P. Koirala*, Bhola Chatterji, p. 75.

Young turk Chandra Shekhar, who in Banaras days used to listen to BP's talks in the 'study circle' was at his bed-side when BP passed away peacefully on 21st July, 1982 in Kathmandu.

7. See Balchandra Sharma, *Nepal Ki Aitihasik Ruprekha*, Banaras, 1951, p. 392.

3

IN THE EYE OF STORM

The ultimate goal of BP's life was to bring democratic socialism to his country with a view to establishing a social system where a common man could aspire with honour for economic, political and soical justice in the society. However, he and his colleagues had felt that unless India got her independence from the British imperialism, it was difficult to bring about such a social transformation in Nepal. Therefore for a long time, BP had made India his battle ground and fought along with the Indian nationalists for India's independence. All such Nepalese in India always had it at the back of their minds that they would eventually have to return to Nepal and start a revolution there. But, it had to be the Indian independence first, for which Nepalese made no small contribution, from Krishna Prasad Koirala's times onwards.

After the World War II, it had become evident that India's independence was not too far. BP had then realised that one part of his mission was accomplished and it was time to turn to the ultimate goal of his life—the people's rule in Nepal. With this resolve, he returned to his own country in 1946.

The first step that he took towards his ultimate goal was to give a clarion call to the people to come together and fight for democracy in Nepal. In this regard he had "...issued a statement (October 1946) regarding the proposed movement which, however, was not published in national dailies". *The Searchlight*, an English language daily from Patna, published it in the form of a letter. A large number of people read this letter and responded to BP's call. Prominent among them were Surya Prasad Upadhyay, who was detained in the Lucknow prison, Dilli Raman Regmi, Krishna Prasad Bhattarai, Balchandra

Sharma, Gopal Prashad Bhattarai, Mahabir Shumsher, Subarna Shumsher, Ganeshman Singh and many others. They started rallying around BP for starting a democratic movement in Nepal. Nepali Sangh of Banaras and Gorkha Congress of Calcutta joined to form Nepal Rastriya Congress for launching a democratic movement in Nepal.

Two preparatory meetings were held—one in Banaras and the other in Calcutta. In January 1947, at Khalsa College in Bhowanipore, Nepali Rastriya Congress was established. The responsibility for Calcutta office was entrusted to D.N.Pradhan, and Banaras office was put under the charge of Gopal Bhattarai. As a mark of respect, Tanka Parsad Acharya of Prajaparisad, who was serving life imprisonment in Kathmandu jail, was nominated as the party President. Balchand Sharma was elected as General Secretary. At the inauguration of Nepali Rastriya Congress, BP moved a resolution which said, "This assembly appreciates Nepal Prajaparisad and its workers for their ideals and zeal. Inspired by a new wave they wanted to bring change in Nepal. But the autocrats cruelly destroyed our jewels. We the members of Nepal Rastriya Congress condemn and openly say those brave sons who suffered and are still suffering in Nepali jails, we demand their immediate release."

The members of the Nepal Prajaparisad who were fighting underground were invited through a resolution to join the Congress in the struggle for bringing about democracy in Nepal. The resolution read, "Because of Nepali Prajaparisad, we are today inaugurating this organisation. There has come about a definite change in the country now. Accordingly we have to change our tactics. This assembly requests the members of Prajaparisad to give up their old ways of underground fight and help us to build up non-violent people's revolution. It is my hope that Nepali Prajaparisad will regard Nepali Rastriya Congress as their own organisation and provide all possible help and support." Among the Indian leaders who had ex-pressed their solidarity with the Nepali Congress and sent greetings to Bhowanipore were Jai Prakash Narayan, Ram Manohar Lohia and Vijaya Lakshmi Pandit.

In March 1947, it was decided to organise the first labour strike in Biratnagar. BP at that time was incharge of the student wing of the Socialist Party of India and was travelling in this connection all over the country. While on his way to Lahore to look into the rift in the student wing there, he got a telegram to proceed to Biratnagar immediately. He was called back because this was going to be the first labour unrest in Nepal and it was thought that his presence was essential.

Those days, Biratnagar had two jute mills, one cotton mill, a sugar factory and a chemical plant. Majority stakes in these mills belonged to the Chamarias of Calcutta but members of Rana family too had sizeable blocks of shares. The jute mill workers, now organised under the banner of Nepali National Congress, went on a strike in 1947. Their demands were reasonable—better service conditions, fair wages, health care, and supply of drinking water in residential areas. Its leadership was provided by Koriala brothers, (Girja Prasad and Tarini Prasad), Man Mohan Adhikari a Communist activist, Yubraj Adhikari and Gehendra Raj. All these were the employees of the jute mill. BP participated in the strike under the banner of the newly formed Nepali National Congress. So did his colleagues like Balchandra Sharma and Gopal Prasad Bhattarai. Not only the leaders, but also the members of their families were arrested. Nepali Rastriya Congress after the arrest of its leaders had an emergency meeting and sent an ultimatum to the Rana Government asking them to put an end to its policy of repression. Later in a conference held in Jogbani (North Bihar) it was decided to launch a civil disobedience movement in Nepal from 13 April 1947. The arrest had created a void in leadership. So, as BP said, "Matrika Prasad Koirala felt called upon to join particularly when Ganesh Man Singh and others urged him to take the leadership after all of them were arrested." M.P. Koirala became the Party President in place of BP and led the movement. After the strike was over, a mass political movement for civil rights, civil liberties and responsible government was started. This was done to build the movement further on the advantages which the labour movement had brought about, i.e., extensive mass awakening. This had given the agitators much needed publicity.

The movement gained some more popularity the way the arrested leaders were taken to the Kathmandu jail. The arrested leaders were made to walk all the way from Biratnagar to Kathmandu. It took nearly three months for the prisoners to cover the distance. In a way, it was exactly what the revolutionaries had wanted. This was a long march in which they traversed hilly areas. On the way, hundreds of people gathered to inquire from these strangers who they were, why they were arrested and what was the objective of the party, the Nepali National Congress, they had formed.

GANDHIJI GOT BP's RELEASE

For over six months BP and some of his colleagues were kept in a house in Kathmandu under strict supervision. BP once again developed the throat trouble. Because of his worsening condition Mahatma Gandhi wrote a letter to the Prime Minister of Nepal Padma Shamsher Jung Bahadur Rana requesting for BP's release. At the same time, Jayaprakash Narayan issued a press statement demanding his immediate release. Dr. Rajendra Prasad sent his book, *India Divided* to BP as a gesture of appreciation. Though many leaders were released after BP's release from the Rana prison, Tarini Prasad and Girja Prasad were detained. They were released only after completing three years of detention.

BP was always popular with the Indian press. The publicity given by the Indian press at that time was extensive. This was something very new for the people living in Kathmandu. Until now they had known only some terrorist activities which were swiftly suppressed by the Rana police and terrorists were often executed without much fanfare. But here was another man, B.P. Koirala, whose arrest had made Mahatma Gandhi to intervene for his release and the whole of Indian press was full of criticism for the barbaric and inhuman treatment given to the Nepalese revolutionaries.

SOME POLITICAL REFORMS ANNOUNCED

Partly, perhaps, democratic movement was gaining ground and partly because the Prime Minister, Padma Shumsher Jung Bahadur Rana had some democratic pretensions, some political reforms were announced in 1947. In his proclamation made on May 16,1947, he declared that he would "constitute a reform committee for Nepal which would suggest changes in the administration so that reforms could be carried out by an Assembly of elected and nominated members". As a first step towards this end, he declared that the elections to the local Panchayats, Municipalities and District boards were to be held within a year. He also gave assurance to establish an independent judicial system, publish annual budget, give grants-in-aid to private schools and establish consulate offices both in India and other friendly countries.

A Reforms Committee with a panel of Indian legal experts was formed. Members were invited to visit Nepal in June 1947. The experts were Sri Prakash, Raghunath Singh and R.V. Singh. The Prime Minister, Padma Shumsher, had some kind of Panchayat constitution in mind. In 1948, the Constitution Reform Committee presented its report to the Prime Minister.

REFORMS FOILED BY MOHAN SHUMSHER

The move towards political awakening were foiled by Mohan Shumsher Jang Bahadur Rana. The reactionary group among the Ranas headed by Mohan Shumsher did not like the democratic moves of Padma Shumsher. Being a powerful group, it forced Padma Shumsher to abdicate in favour of Mohan Shumsher in April 1948. But before his forced retirement, Padma Shumsher promulgated on 26th January 1948 the Government of Nepal Act 2004 which came to be known as first Constitution of Nepal. Mohan Shumsher quickly imposed a reign of terror. People with any connection with the reformist movement were rearrested and tortured.

BP and his friends, Krishna Prasad Bhattarai and Kedarman Byathit, who had fled the country, once again entered Nepal incognito and started organising the people. All the three went to Jayanagar through Darbhanga. With the help of Bodh Prasad Upadhyaya, they took Siduli *chor* trek (trek of the thieves) crossing mountains and rivers reached Dumja, in disguise. Whatever they had carried till then was left on the mountains of Dumja. Now they proceeded towards Kathmandu, again in disguise. In a coarse Labeda Surual (Nepali dress), a faded cap and coat, a big tilak on his forehead, BP had taken the guise of a priest. He had a muffler around his neck and one old white spectacles. Kedarman disguised as a petty businessman and K.P. Bhattarai with a Sanskrit book *Kaumudi* under his arm looked typical Sanskrit scholar. They entered Kathmandu and started organising the people alongside the underground members of the Prajaparisad. BP, disguised as a priest, rented a cycle and started instigating people in different areas. He would often go to Dharhara to 'Mahilas cheya pasal' (tea shop) to have tea and meet people.

He often met the members of Prajaparisad and told them, 'a movement only in Kathmandu will not be sufficient; it has to spread to the whole of the country'. He invited Prajaparisad leaders to represent the Sammelan (meeting) which he planned to organise in Banaras. Some of the members of Prajaparisad however preferred to stay in Kathmandu. They said, "you go and organise there, we will work here. We all will benefit by your strength. Our strength will be yours and yours ours."

ARRESTED AGAIN AND TORTURED

Within a month BP was back in prison. Mohan Shumsher, now determined to crush all revolts, resorted to coercive tactics. BP was kept in unimaginably horrible conditions. It was winter. He did not have adequate clothes, nor a pair of shoes. For, when the police had surrounded the house where he was staying, he did not have time to put on his jacket and shoes in trying to escape the arrest. In jail, he was not given any clothes. He was instead handcuffed and put in fetters with a chain around his waist. A military guard kept a twenty-four-hour watch on him. On the third night, he lost his consciousness. In spite of all kinds of threats and torture, the Rana military could not extract a confession or any information from him, nor could they locate his contacts in Kathmandu. When all the pressures failed they packed him to a solitary confinement and gave him an inhuman treatment.

He was kept in a room that was so unhygienic that, according to the doctors, "nobody could survive living in those rooms."

B.P. Koirala with his wife Sushila Koirala, Jaya Mani Dixit
and Rani Rebati Devi

Smt. Indira Gandhi, Rani Rebati Devi and Sushila Koirala, wife of B.P. Koirala.

Smt. Indira Gandhi, Sushila Koirala (wife of BP) with Pandit Jawaharlal Nehru, B.P. Koirala and Dr. Gopal Swarup Pathak, Vice President of India.

In fact, the room in which he was kept was one of the rooms used to store firewood. His room had been repaired, enforced with cement. The roof was very low and dripping wet. The room was about eight feet by eleven and had a small hole in the centre which was supposed to serve as a latrine. There were three bricks in a corner which was to be his kitchen. He was provided with a small cot of wet timber and an old carpet. The room was so dark that he felt 'it was a dungeon'. It had a small passage for skylight with a grill, but it was permanently closed. The jailor had come on the first morning to tell BP that he would be given three *pau* (approximately three quarters of a kilogram) rice not properly husked, one paisa, three chillies, some salt and a bundle of firewood. BP was kept there for six months during which he did not see a human face. He had lost count of the days.

HOW BP KEPT IN TOUCH WITH OUTSIDE WORLD

On one day in his solitary confinement, BP heard a guard singing. He could instinctively make out that there was a man who could help him out in the prison. He started talking to the guard. After some initial hesitation, the Gurung guard became friendly. On BP's request, he brought a small piece of pencil and a wrapper of a book. BP wrote a letter to Pandit Jawaharlal Nehru on that wrapper. That letter was taken by Krishna Prasad Bhattarai and Balchander Sharma to Pandit Nehru. He said, "Panditji was visibly moved and became tearful on reading it."

One day, BP requested the jailor to get a proper *chulha* (fire place) made in his room as he was sick of eating gruel day in and day out. The jailor granted his request. So a proper *chulha* was made. BP managed to hide his precious possession—a pencil and a few sheets of paper in the hollow of the *chulha*. When the authorities came to search his cell, they could find nothing. This is how he kept his contact with his friends in India and Nepal.

BP ON HUNGER STRIKE

In spite of his contacts with the Indian leaders, BP continued to languish in jail. The inhuman treatment given to him and his failing health forced him to go on his historic hunger strike on Akshay Tritia day in 1949. The Ranas thought this event could be kept secret but they were mistaken. On the eighth day of the hunger strike, BP's condition turned serious. His brothers, Tarini and Girja Prasad Koirala, who were still behind the bars since the jute mill strike, were summoned. The Prime Minister, Girja Prasad Koirala, recalling those horrifying days said: "We were in Nakhu jail. BP was kept in Hari Shumsher's *tabela* (stable), we got the message that BP was on a hunger strike, in an interesting way. Our jail doctor sent us a bottle of black liquid medicine. We were quite surprised to get it because neither of us had asked for any medicine. On emptying the bottle we found a small paper which had this message. At first we did not know what to do. We thought of joining him on fast. To this we got the message from BP not to do so. Those were tense days....Later when his condition really started worsening, Mohan Shumsher sent Chandra Bahadur and Narendra Mani Dixit to us. We were taken to BP. By this act, we could infer that the Government was yielding to pressure."

BP's brothers were asked by the authorities to persuade him to give up his hunger strike. But his brothers acted otherwise. They pretended that they were seriously persuading their brother to give up the fast and co-operate with the authorities. But, in fact, they served as link between BP and outside leaders. BP was conveyed the message that "[he] should continue with [his] hunger strike." They also informed him that tremendous pressure against the Ranas was being built in Nepal and India. Sooner or later the Ranas would bow down. Everyday they were brought to jail and everyday BP, due to their messages, got renewed will-power to resist. One day they brought him clothes and for the first time bathed him properly. When BP's condition started deteriorating further, his brothers were stopped from meeting him. There was no more news about his health. The Ranas just kept silent. There was silence from all sides, a silence too oppressive for Shushila, BP's wife. Now it was her turn to take the initiative. She contacted Jai Prakash Narayan, who was hospitalised in Patna because of an accident. From his hospital bed, JP contacted Panditji and entreated him to save BP's life.

Panditji sent a telegram to Mohan Shumsher and asked Shushila to proceed to Kathmandu. Since the Ranas had issued an arrest warrant against her one-year-old son, Prakash, she could not proceed immediately. Once again Pandit Nehru intervened. He asked the Bihar government to provide an aeroplane for her to be taken to Kathmandu. But this was frustrated by the scheming Ranas on the ground that Gauchar airport was not cemented and therefore it was not possible for them to give orders for the plane to land. Finally, Shushila with her small son went by road to Kathmandu. She was joined by BP's mother, Dibyadevi. Sushila arrived in Kathmandu on the 24th day of her husband's hunger strike. It happened to be Tuesday. Following a social custom in Nepal, one does not meet one's near and dear ones after a long separation on Tuesday. At best one has to wait till sunset.

BP's MOTHER ADMONISHED THE PRIME MINISTER

Dibyadevi, by now an old woman, went to see her son in jail who was struggling for life. When the officials asked her to stay in jail to take care of her son, she refused and said defiantly, "No, as long as he is not released he will be under the care of the government. The government must be responsible for him". When the doctor attending on BP insisted, she impudently refused," not in prison". Due to her insistence, there was no alternative left. So both mother and wife were taken to the Prime Minister. In the presence of Mohan Shumsher's younger son, Vijaya Shumsher, Dibyadevi faced the Prime Minister boldly and said,"I consigned my husband's body to the fire (his body was taken from Rana jail to Arya Ghat, the cremation ground in Kathmandu) and I have come to put my son's body on fire."

This was the same, shy, hesitant and beautiful Dibyadevi of her early Banaras days. Life had taught her many lessons which had hardened her attitude towards life. She was destined to hold steadfast to the right and just cause. Dibyadevi now was prepared to sacrifice her son's life for the same cause for which her husband Krishna Prasad had laid down his life. After listening to her, Mohan Shumsher said, "How can the Government yield to the pressure of an obstinate young man? The Government has its own prestige to preserve." Promptly came her reply, "What is your prestige compared to my son's prestige?" Mohan Shumsher was so agitated that he turned to his son, Vijaya, and said, "I knew I would receive such replies. It is you who insisted that I should meet them."

After this meeting, Mohan Shumsher's Secretary, Narendra Mani Dixit went to *dharmashala* (guest house) where the Koiralas were staying. Narendra Mani Dixit was also related to Dibyadevi. The moment she saw him, she charged, "You have remembered us after twenty years. Now, I no more recognise you as my relative; I regard you an emissary of Mohan Shumsher. Tell me what you have come here for, what do you want?" He had no answer.

RELEASE FROM THE JAIL AND AFTER

On the twenty-ninth day of this historic hunger strike, BP was released unconditionally from his captivity. It was a moral victory for non-violence. Its impact on the minds of ordinary citizen of Nepal was enormous. After his release, BP introspected regarding his political philosophy. BP had this to say: "Gandhi, Marx and then again Gandhi. I began with Gandhi, had an interlude of Marx, and then returned to Gandhi...." During his hunger strike, BP came to realize that path of non-violent mass movement must be amended. In Kathmandu he found that the people were not responding to their call for non-violent Satyagraha. "My own non-violence was always a matter of tactics than an article of faith. But until you have a sword how can you go to the battlefield? I consider Gandhi a greater original thinker than Marx. Marx was a product, he was not an original thinker. He stood on the shoulders of others. But Gandhi was original."

By the time BP was released, he had become so weak that he could not be removed from the four walls of the prison. All restrictions were, however, lifted and the Prime Minister's own physician used to come every day to examine him. BP was now looked after well. During this period, BP and Mohan Shumsher had developed an understanding for each other's point of view.

This had a lasting effect on BP's mind. They continued to show the understanding of each other's point of view in the most trying situations.

History was soon to take a turn when BP would be called to join the first coalition government formed under the Prime Ministership of Mohan Shumsher in 1951. According to BP, Mohan Shumsher was a kind-hearted and a religious man. It was circumstances which had made him his adversary and contender for power. BP's opinion about his adversary also shows that he was above petty politics and personal jealousies. BP used to say that "every man howsoever bad he might be, has a streak of goodness in him and it depends on the quality of a leader to bring that hidden goodness out."

On the twelfth day after he broke his fast, BP was called by the Prime Minister at midnight. In front of his two sons (Sarada Shumsher and Vijaya Shumsher) and Secretary Narendra Mani Dixit, Mohan Shumsher told BP that he was released not because of any pressure from Nehru or other Indian friends of his, but because he did not want the death of a Brahmin to remain on his conscience. He also said, "You are a free man now, go and enjoy your life. You are in bad health, so go to your doctor in Bombay or elsewhere. But never be under the illusion that we will handover power to you. Power is given to one, the right to possess power is written here (indicating his forehead)."

BP's release from the jail raises a question of academic interest: was BP released from jail because of Mohan Shumsher's fear that if a Brahmin died under his custody he would fall under the curse of *brahmhatya* (the murder of a Brahmin) or was it due to the pressure of Pandit Nehru's letter? This question can be answered in the light of Mohan Shumsher's reaction to a somewhat similar case. Swami Shankaran, another Nepali Congress functionary, was arrested for distributing Congressite phamphlet. He too had gone on a hunger strike. When the jailor informed the Prime Minister that Swami's condition was becoming quite critical, the Prime Minister was reported to have said, "I am waiting for his death, let him die. He is not a Koirala that Nehru will intervene. I want him to die a dog's death," and Swami died a martyr's death. This shows that BP was released from the jail mainly due to the pressure brought on the Prime Minister by Pandit Nehru, rather than the fear of *brahmhatya*. Later, Gopal Prasad Upadhyaya, Purna Bahadur, Surya Bahadur and Shiv Deo had all to resort to hunger strike for demands of elementary nature, but were not released for this kind of fear.

BP's 'Karishma' was built on small but solid instances. Much later however the national reconciliation policy adopted by BP turned the tide. Because of massive consciousness created for pro-democratic forces, many people from the opposite camp started rallying around BP. It is interesting to note that even those who had demanded BP's execution came to join him under his banner. According to Hari Bhattarai, presently manager of Nepal-Arab Bank, narrated this story: "During hey days of Panchayat, many Panches took upon themselves the responsibility of issuing decree that BP should be hanged." In Palpa district Shobha Sakya, chairperson of the district level women's organisation passed a resolution advocating confirmation of this verdict. In the changed atmosphere, Shobha Sakya too was in a queue to meet BP. Nepali Congress workers objected and said she should not be allowed to meet BP. When BP heard this controversy, he smiled in his characteristic way and said, "Come to think of it, I have changed the mind of my adversary, don't you think it is a political victory. If she has decided to fight for our cause what is the harm in meeting her." This not only pacified his followers but also people like Hari became life-long admirers of BP.

It was this belief that had led BP to seek an audience with the Prime Minister earlier — when he had visited Kathmandu incognito. He had sought the help of the Indian Ambassador, Surjeet Singh Majithia, in this regard. Majithia promised that he could get the appointment but could not take the responsibility for his safety. To this BP said, "Unless you can guarantee my safety what is the purpose of my asking you to work as go between." BP's idea was to place a few minimum demands like civil liberties, freedom of association and freedom of speech for Mohan Shumsher's consideration.

At the midnight meeting before his release, the Prime Minister assured him that his government would carry out democratic reforms. Indeed it was because of that assurance that BP issued the following statement in a press conference:

Nepal's politics must be viewed in the Asian context where a great shift in the seat of power is taking place. Thanks to the impact of the last Great War and the sudden disappearance of a mighty foreign power that was dominating over India and also over the politics of South East Asia for the last two centuries, politics of Nepal has come of age all too suddenly. There is an acute economic distress under which generations of our people have been groaning. This permanent famine is not a result of any acts of god such as cessation of rains, flood etc; for this appalling distress unresponsive administration must share the major portion of responsibility. Whereas before the great war, people submitted to the denial of essentials of life in a spirit of resignation, the post-war Nepali has been imbibed with the spirit of the new times. The distress must end. Behind the din and bustle of politics looms this great factor of economics. Masses are concerned with food, clothing and shelter which have become progressively unavailable to them, but to the sensitive educated Nepali, apart from anything else, unresponsive Government is too much of a burden. Therefore, there is hardly a section in the population of Nepal that is satisfied with the state of things obtaining there. A general discontent is seething underground. Loyalty of the Services and the Army is also gradually being affected. The stepmotherly treatment that Tarai people have been receiving at the hands of the Government is another factor contributing to the extreme discontent prevailing among the people of Nepal. It is no wonder therefore that in Nepal situation is pregnant with dangerous possibilities. If nothing is done to give satisfaction to the people immediately, our country will go to the camp of anarchy and chaos.

Asia is passing through a momentous period of great transition. Change is overtaking us everywhere; somewhere the process is accompanied with extreme violence, civil war and appalling blood-spilling, and in other places the process is comparatively peaceful. It is in this background that our decision to suspend the Satyagraha must be judged. We of the Nepali National Congress want to take the course of peace, but if the Government do not make an appropriate gesture, our efforts at peaceful advancement of the country will come to naught. After all, discontent must find an outlet and expression. If the Government do not permit democratic forces to develop, terrorism, violence and forces of evil are bound to raise their heads. In actual fact the delay in granting simple political rights to the people has already thrown a large number of young men into the camp of fascism and such organisations as have scant respect for democracy. What is happening in China, Burma, Malaya, and other places has given a fillip to the thought in Nepal that Gandhian method of non-violence is unsuited for a country like Nepal where Government has ruthlessly suppressed all vestiges of democracy.

After my release I had a long talk with the Maharaja and on my presentation of the people's point of view to him, he seemed to be genuinely anxious to do something to ease the situation. Though he was not prepared to commit himself to the fulfilment of our demands which were the basis for the last Satyagraha movement, he left me in no doubt that Government would concede them if they got a breathing space. Moreover, when an opening has been made for real understanding between the Government and the people, we must do everything to promote it rather than hinder the process. To the impatient critics of our decision to postpone the movement, my reply is: time is in our favour; time given to the Government is so much time gained for us and not for those who are trying to halt the march of history. When the politics of Nepal has come of age, it does not behove us to behave impatiently and petulantly. I have every hope that the Government would reciprocate this unmistakable gesture from our side, but if they are so ill-counselled as not to do it, we reserve to ourselves the right to choose a different course of action.

BP FRUSTRATED AGAIN

When for months nothing happened, BP expressed his frustration and bitterness saying that "hoping for reforms from the selfish Ranas was like hoping for milk from a dry cow. Nepali Rastriya Congress accused Mohan Shumsher of pursuing a ruthless policy."

Nepal saw Satyagraha for the first time in 1950. BP issued a statement which said, "Mass Satygraha has been launched in several parts of Nepal and in Parasi district a regular civil disobedience movement is on. Kisans are courting arrest in hundreds....The political ferment has also affected the military of Kathmandu. Seventeen army Officers have been put under arrest for showing sympathies to Nepali Congress. They are kept in strict isolation in the Prime Minister's palace".

The difference of opinion between different political parties was only helping Ranas. It was perhaps this situation which called for the merger of two parties, viz., Nepal Prajatantrik Congress and Nepali National Congress. The most trusted friend and comrade of BP, Krishna Prasad Bhattarai said, "In late 1948 BP was arrested in Kathmandu. I was with him, but escaped the Rana police and secretly returned to Jainagar. It was during this period that we began contemplating merger with Nepal Prajatantrik Congress. The latter also reciprocated willingly by attending our merger talks. On our part the factors which influenced the move, everyone was feeling at that time disunity and differences in the democratic camps would yield no results. In fact public opinion was greatly in favour of unity of the two parties."

"We were always short of funds and this handicapped our organisational and agitational works. The Nepal Prajatantrik Congress had better and more regular contacts with Kathmandu valley than we had. It was a more militant organisation that had proposed merger with Nepali Rastriya Congress".

BP by now was convinced that Ranas would not listen to reason. The Nepal Prajatantrik Congress neither had a working cadre nor a definite political outlook. Its only objective was the end of Rana autocracy in Nepal. He realised that the merger of the two parties would strengthen the democratic movement.

The historic merger took place in Patna on 17th March, 1950. The resolution adopted on this occasion read,"In the interest of unity among progressive forces in Nepal so that with their combined efforts democracy may be installed there at the earliest date, our working committees have recommended a merger of the two organizations. We feel that the unification of the Nepali National Congress and Nepal Democratic Congress will pave the way for coming in of the common organization of other groups and individuals, who are actuated by the same objective of democracy in Nepal. Both these organizations have decided that the country should be prepared for the fight to the finish against the autocracythat has no parallel anywhere in its ruthlessness."

BP's reaction on the merger was, "All patriots and well-wishers of Nepal will rejoice at this news. So long as the national forces of progress remain disjoined, the feudal tyranny of Nepal will continue to flourish, to exploit the people, to subject them to inhuman conditions of living. It is this consciousness that has brought the two premier organizations of our country together with the united force the people will fight better."

A meeting was held in Baigania in Bihar near Indo-Nepalese border within five months of the merger. It was decided to launch a liberation movement in Nepal. It was a momentous decision. BP wanted that the battle for democracy in Nepal be fought on the soil of Nepal. He said, "From the reports of the units it was now evident that Nepalese masses are ready for action. It would be suicidal to continue from foreign land anymore. Entry into Nepal of the organisational set up was urgently called for."

KING FLED THE COUNTRY

It was also the time when trouble was brewing in the royal family. A conspiracy was unearthed in which some top ranking Ranas were involved. They wanted to overthrow Mohan Shumsher from the Prime Ministership. Due to this incident Ranas got distracted. Meanwhile, King Tribhuvan got the opportunity to escape.

With all but one member of his family, King Tribhuvan left the royal palace and took shelter in the Indian Embassy in Kathmandu on November 6, 1950. After four days of stay there, he left for New Delhi where he received a hero's welcome. Immediately after the Nepalese Prime Minister convened a Bharadari Sabha consisting of nobility, Raj Gurus and Bharadars of the state to consider this issue. They declared "unanimously and emphatically in writing that according to the laws, usage, and the constitution of Nepal Maharajadhiraja Tribhuvan Bir Bikram Shah Deva and the ... members of the royal family had by their action, forfeited their right to the throne."

ARMED STRUGGLE

While the Rana family was in turmoil, the volunteers of the Nepali Congress launched the liberation struggle. Three hundred armed volunteers of the Nepali Congress made a surprise attack in Birganj, captured the governor and other officials and set up an independent government. The Nepali Congress liberation forces, now called the 'Mukti Sena', attacked other places too. An assault on Biratnagar, however, failed due to stiff resistance from the royal troops. In the western Nepal, Parasi was captured under the leadership of Dr. K.I. Singh. There were quite a few cases of loot and arson, murder of zamindars and moneylenders. However, Mukti Sena could never have defeated the well trained Rana troops. Neither did the hope of the revolutionaries materialise that once the opportunity was provided a number of royal soldiers would walk over to their side.

Besides, Mukti Sena did not have sufficient supply of arms and ammunition. Their's was a dare devil attempt. It succeeded however in opening the floodgates for spontaneous popular protests and demonstrations which rocked Nepal. The Rana police failed to suppress this upsurge.

DELHI INTERVENED

The political upsurge, the moral support which Mukti Sena got from the fugitive king at Delhi and the stand taken by the Indian Government broke the morale of the Ranas. On December 6th, 1950 Pandit Jawaharlal Nehru reiterated that "India would continue to give recognition to King Tribhuvan as the head of the state". The Indian Government in the meanwhile submitted a memorandum on 8th December 1950 to the Rana Prime Minister. It suggested that some constitutional reform measures be taken up immediately. A Constituent Assembly should be convened which should include persons enjoying public confidence, even members of the Rana family should be included. The King Tribhuvan should continue as king in the interest of the country. Later, with some changes, it came to be known as Delhi Agreement. The fleeing of the King had drawn the attention of the whole world to the happenings in the Himalayan kingdom.

On 16th January 1951, M.P. Koirala, President of the Nepali Congress, called for cessation of all operations by the Congress volunteers in Nepal and appealed to everyone to assist in the restoration of peace". Referring to the cease-fire appeal of Matrika Prasad Koirala, BP said, "It is obvious that unless there is cessation of hostilities on both sides, there can be no proper climate for negotiations"... He further said, "We shall participate in the negotiations, free from any commitments whatsoever. We have always stood for unadulterated democracy in Nepal and this objective will guide us during all the stages of negotiations.

M. P. Koirala the President of the Nepali Congress, B. P. Koirala and Suvarna Shumsher came to Delhi on January 14, 1950 at the invitation of the Government of India and held discussions on the issue arising out of the declaration made by the Prime Minister of Nepal on January 8th, 1950.

The old order collapsed by its own weight. Due to intervention and mediation of the Government of India, King Tribhuvan returned and set up a new order. A coalition government consisting of representatives of the Ranas and the Nepali Congress was set up. King Tribhuvan, after negotiations, issued a proclamation which severely limited the scope and authority of the council of ministers and made the position of the King secure. It laid down that the ministers would hold office as long as the King wanted. The council of ministers would remain collectively responsible to the Monarch for their actions. Later he said, "The ... ministers shall hold office during our pleasure and shall jointly be responsible to us". Thus, the change that took place in Nepal was not a revolution but the restoration of the dynastic rule of the Shah King which their ancestor, Surendra Bikram Shah had handed over to Jang Bahadur Rana and his successors in 1894. This game went unnoticed by BP and the Nepali Congress during those euphoric days of the 'victory'.

The political situation in Nepal, immediately after the overthrow of the Rana regime, was characterised by three players, namely, (a) the monarch, (b) the landed aristocracy, and (c) the popular elements represented by the political parties, especially the Nepali Congress. Among these, the monarch enjoyed enormous power and prestige. He was the head of the entire administration in the country and people loved him for his daring act. Now the Ranas were the direct target of people's wrath. The king as earlier projected by the Ranas was regarded as the source of strength and a living incarnation of Vishnu—the Hindu God of preservation. In a country where religion still remains a driving force, the reasons for the king's towering personality and prominence are not difficult to understand.

King Tribhuvan's participation in anti-Rana movement and fleeing the country, enhanced the crown's prestige. The King indirectly had shown keen interest in the activities of the revolutionaries. By the sheer force of events, he had become a part of the movement. The King became the symbol of nationalism and all other qualities needed for the birth of modern democratic Nepal. The unstable conditions of the country and the repeated breakdown of the administrative authority since 1951 helped the King to add effective power to his newly acquired prestige. In the absence of a strong political party and organised democratic forces, the common man began to believe that the King alone could wield authority and give them peace and prosperity which none of the leaders seemed capable of providing.

MOVEMENT FOR DEMOCRACY WEAKENED

After the restoration of his throne, King Tribhuvan concentrated on capturing administrative powers. No measure was taken to end feudal land ownership or to reorganise the economy to provide better conditions to the peasantry. The major sections of the society were not with the Nepali Congress. Resistance to change came from the vested interests and in the ensuing dispute, the King never actively sided with the reformers. This has been the tragedy of Nepal. The democratic forces failed to understand the role and character of the rejuvenated monarchy at first. It escaped their notice that the King's participation in the revolution was due mainly to the force of circumstances and sooner or later the role of the King was bound to give way to the reactionary forces.

After the formation of the Rana-Congress ministry, some sections of the Nepali Congress were disillusioned. Explaining to them, BP presented in 1952 a solution to resolve inter-party differences. It said:

> If there had been some other party in power our task would have been clear. Like the opposition parties we would trail for Governmental mistakes and agitate whenever such mistakes are made. But since our party is in power that distinct independence cannot be had.

> We have to note that this government is our government. Its works and mistakes are partly ours too. We cannot be destructive in our attitude towards it. We shall help in its good works, but those which are unjust we shall criticise too. Our responsibility is not easy.

> On this basis we reach two working principles. Our organisation is distinct from the government. One responsibility is to run the administration, but other being activities outside it are still more important. It is necessary to keep, as much as possible, unity between the work inside the government, but if there is any conflict between the two we shall give importance to outside work. We share our right to conduct agitation.

> The Congress has to perform today the task of a parliament... So long as the parliament is not elected our slogan is, 'let Congress work as parliament'. It is the duty of the party to put into practice the above principles. The present kind of

weaknesses of the organisation will make it fail to carry out its historical responsibility.

However in spite of BP's efforts, the democratic forces in Nepal could not gather momentum. The lack of maturity of Nepali politicians, their constant intrigues and scramble for power never permitted the popular forces to merge into effective unit against their enemies. In the resulting rigmarole of group politics and pettiness, the larger goals of economic and political reforms were completely forgotten. Instead, there was a general scramble by the politicians to gain the favour of the Monarch. Some of them succeeded in entering the ministry. This only strengthened the Royal hands. Average Nepali became more and more apathetic towards politics and political parties in general. In view of this trend, the meeting of the working committee of the Nepali Congress held from 10th to 13th March 1953 passed a Resolution:

> It resolves that since the present reactionary Government is driving the people for popular action against it, a sub-committee consisting of Messers B.P. Koirala, Subrna Shumsher, Surya Prasad Upadhyay, Ganesh Man Singh and Mahendra Narain Nidhi be formed, charged with the responsibility of the preparation of a programme of action. The Mahasamiti will soon be called to secure its sanction for launching of a popular movement."

REFERENCES

1. *Gorakhapatra*, 47 (4 Jaith 2004 Vs) 1,4.
2. During his short tenure as Prime Minister of Nepal, BP, while passing through Delli-Bazar, saw the same Gurung Sentry in a shop. BP asked the driver to stop the car. He recognised BP. He told him, now he has a small farm where he worked... and also had got married. BP gave his address and requested him to come to his house. Gurung never visited him. BP could never forget this man who had helped him out of that predicament.
3. *Nepal Today*, July, 1950, Calcutta, p. 6.
4. *Ibid.*, 5 March, 1949.
5. *Ibid.*, p. 6.
6. Interview with Anirudha Gupta, "Nepali Politics: A Decade of Doldrum, 1951-1961", unpublished monograph, p. 57.

7. "On unity and thereafter B.P. Koirala" *Nepal Today*, March-April, 1950, 12-13 issue, p. 5, Calcutta.
8. *Ibid.*
9. *Nepal Today*, March-April, 1950.
10. Government of Nepal, Department of Publicity, Bulletin, No. 28, Government of Nepal Communique Regarding King Tribhuvan's Abdication, Nov. 7, 1950.
11. *Jawaharlal Nehru Speeches*, 57, p. 177.
12. *Hindu*, 17 Jan. 1951.
13. *Hindu*, 19 Jan. 1951.
14. The Interim Government Nepal Act proclaimed by Tribhuvan on March, 1951.
15. King Tribhuvan's Historic Proclamation of 18 February 1957, initiating the age of reform. *Hindu*, Madras, 20 February, 1957.
16. B.P. Koirala, Nepali Congress and Government Biratnagar, 1952.
17. Nepali Congress Central Office, Kathmandu, Nepal, 1953.

4

ROYAL STRUGGLE FOR POWER AND POLITICAL STALEMATE

The political environment of Nepal in the 1950s was characterized by constant political changes : changes in the government, splits, mergers and disintegration of political groups and parties. It was a decade of political stalemate and economic stagnation. Why and how these things happened? Why especially, a political revolution which had promised to revolutionize the life and condition of the people of Nepal petered out in an unbelievable quandry?

WHY AND HOW IT HAPPENED ?

The Delhi Agreement was a compromise between the King, the Nepali Congress and the Ranas. It gave the country an interim constitution and guaranteed democratic rights to the people. However, it could not wipe out the discontent among the different groups. Some dubbed it as "infamous" and others called it as "total surrender to Indian pressure." Referring to the Delhi Agreement, BP says "I don't think it is fair to dub the Delhi Agreement infamous." As a matter of fact, it laid the foundation of democracy in Nepal. Even to this day, the agreement—along with the Royal Proclamation issued by the late King Tribhuvan on Feb. 18, 1951—serves as the starting point for all debates on freedom and democracy in Nepal.[1] However, Ranas' hostility to it was open. There were others like Dr. K.I. Singh, who refused to lay down arms for they thought Delhi Agreement a betrayal of the people. The Communists of Nepal had habitually to oppose any move taken by the Nepali Congress. It is also true that the Nepali Congress too could not make full use of the revolutionary fervour created by the armed struggle of 1950-51. Within two months of the formation of a new coalition government, obscurantic tactics of the Prime Minister Mohan Shumsher and other Rana ministers made it clear to the Congress that it was impossible for them to put their economic reforms programme into practice. As a result, the Congress ministers resigned en bloc from the cabinet. The next day Rana group had to follow suit.

King Tribhuvan's participation in the anti-Rana movement had enhanced the prestige of the crown. During the course of their long despotic rule, the Ranas themselves had reared up a tradition of monarchy and its divine theory which later paved the way for their downfall. The tug-of-war for power between the Crown and the Congress leadership continued. BP says: "On question for power the king did not want to relent. In fact he wanted to get more power for himself, for the crown, for the king, whereas I wanted that the king should start functioning as a constitutional monarch right from the onset...". There is no doubt King Tribhuvan's participation gave moral support and success to the Nepali Congress. Its prestige was enhanced by this support. This was of some importance as the Ranas were still very powerful. On every conceivable occasion, they worked to discredit the Nepali Congress as a bunch of usurpers having somehow managed to mislead the people. Only Ranas could rule. The King, being reinstated, realised for the first time the luring effect of power. He started taking active part in the political life of Nepal. India, as usual always pressed to take a role of a peace maker, would once in a while try to impress the Congress leadership for all kinds of omissions and commissions.

On March 30, 1951, the Interim Constitution of Nepal Act 2007 was enforced. It was definitely a break from the past. It was the first attempt to bring about a change in Nepal for social equity, justice and political freedom. Because of this a Rana extremist group started organising the Gorkha Dal, better known as Khukri Dal, with avowed belief in violent methods. Sensing the danger, BP then the Home Minister, passed an order and declared Gorkha Dal an illegal organisation on 15 April, 1951. Many of the Gorkha Dal leaders were arrested. On that ill-fated day, a crowd of members of Gorkha Dal broke open the prison gates and secured the release of their leaders.

The mob then started moving towards the residence of the Home Minister. BP was with his friends when the crowd pushed in. Giving a graphic description of the event that followed, Prime Minister Girja Prasad Koirala recalled, "This friend of BP was tall and was staying in the front room. The Khukri Dal members came in, they had not yet seen BP. The moment they saw this friend they started shouting and were about to strike him with a Khukri. BP then stood in front and said, "I am BP." The crowd moved forward to strike him". BP moving in the corner of the door started firing, killing some of them. Gradually the crowd dispersed. By then the Mukti Sena volunteers arrived and the situation was brought under control. BP, a believer in non-violence, also knew that situations like these could not be tackled by non-violent means. It was true that violence had its backlash but when peaceful and other constitutional means failed, the people have every right to resort to other means. He was never dogmatic about ideology or class, caste, hierarchy and injustices. With him the gap between what he said and practised was never too wide. This is what had touched the heart of a common man of Nepal.

BP had earlier started reorganising Mukti Sena into a people's militia known as Raksha Dal to counter the military threats of the Ranas. Meanwhile the food situation in the country was getting worse. King Tribhuvan announced on October 2, 1951 an Advisory Assembly of 35 persons to assist and advise the Government.[2] Mohan Shumsher publicly questioned the King's right to do so. BP and the Congress countered that Mohan Shumsher was challenging the King's authority. This was understandable when the fight was with the Ranas but when King Tribhuvan started asserting more and more power for himself Nepali Congress leaders could do nothing about it. On November 6, a group of Raksha Dal soldiers opened fire on a procession of students in Kathmandu. This incident was naturally used by Mohan Shumsher to tarnish the image of the Home Minister. On 10th November 1951, BP declared over the Nepal Radio that reactionary forces were making a bid to stage a comeback. These chaotic conditions led to the demise of the coalition government.

After the fall of the coalition government, the King invited Shri Matrika Prasad Koirala to form the government. The palace had started contriving to usurp more and more power for itself. Matrika Prasad Koirala ascended the seat of power as Prime Minister in his capacity as President of the Nepali Congress. He unfortunately allowed himself to be used by the palace in throttling the spirit of the Nepali revolution. The differences between the new Prime Minister and his party colleagues deepened every day. In July 1952, Nepali Congress Working Committee asked Matrika Prasad Koirala to reorganize his cabinet and reduce the membership from eleven to seven. Matrika Prasad Koirala refused to do so. As a result, he and his supporters were expelled from the Working Committee. This had to happen because, unlike BP, Matrika Prasad depended on the King's mercy for strength. "Much that happened during this period is of no historical consequence. But one clear fact that emerges from the din and confusion is that the palace gained much through him at the cost of the nascent democracy and that after his severance from the Congress he was converted into nothing more than an instrument of manoeuvre of the palace."[3]

Matrika Prasad said that 'the king was not only a reigning monarch, he was a ruling one', implying thereby that during the interim period prior to the formation of a popular government through elections, constitutional monarchy was inoperative. Furthermore, while the party wanted to undertake reforms speedily, he held that 'major reforms were the responsibility of future, and not of the present period of transition'. Matrika Prasad Koirala's political conservatism was the bone of contention between the Koirala brothers.

It is noteworthy that "In defiance of all democratic conventions and practices, the King demonstrated his partisan attitude by calling upon him (M.P. Koirala) to form the Government again and again. He was commissioned as the President of Nepali Congress, then as the President of another party which he hurriedly formed, a National Coalition Government after his expulsion from the Congress, then again in his individual capacity, to form one Government after another. What was sacrificed in the process was the spirit of democracy".[4] The differences between 'thulo daju' (elder brother) Matrika Prasad Koirala and BP had so much widened that Jai Prakash Narayan had to intervene. A settlement was reached and press statement issued which said, "a member who indulges in propaganda against either of us in future will be disclaimed by us jointly and, if neccessary, disciplinary action will be taken against him."[5]

INFIGHTING WITHIN THE CONGRESS

On the other hand, the things at the democratic front were not in order. The tussle for power within the Congress party was also apparent. After the postponement of Satyagraha, D.R. Regmi was elected president by a delegates' conference. Later, BP challenged the validity of his election and asked Regmi to resign. Dr. Regmi refused to resign and, shortly afterwards, quit the party along with his followers. Despite the continuous depletion in its ranks, the Nepali Congress remained the largest political organisation in the country. After the fall of the coalition government, BP started organising mass movement with the sole objective of compelling the monarch to hold free and fair elections. The leaders of Nepali Congress issued a statement asking for early general elections, an independent judiciary, independent audit and accounts system, a public service commission, freedom of speech.[6] At the Sixth National Conference (January 1956), the party had issued a new manifesto calling for the achievement of socialism by peaceful and democratic means.

The manifesto reiterated party's faith in achieving socialism by gradual elimination of feudal relations in land and rapid industrialization. The land policy included abolition of the big Birta, a sort of zamindari system. It envisaged a ceiling on land holding and distribution of excess land, in due course, to the landless peasants.

To understand the land problem we will have to briefly go back into the history of Nepal. It is well known that Prithvi Narayan Shah of Gorkha had consolidated Nepal into a state during the 18th century.[7] He provided a lasting social order and consolidated small principalities into a cohesive unit. Once this was accomplished, it logically followed that all land in Nepal was regarded as the property of the state. The administrative staff were given tax-free land called *birtas* and *Jagir* in lieu of payments for the services rendered to the crown. Prithvi Narayan Shah had also distributed tax-free land to the Brahmins and Guthi land for rendering religious services to the temples. Later, Rana Bahadur started persecuting the Brahmins because they had opposed his despotic rule, and confiscated Guthi lands on the plea that they 'forfeited the right of their caste by unworthiness of their conduct.'[8]

During this period, Nepalese court, like everywhere else, was characterized by intrigues. On the 14th September 1846, a minister, who was a favourite of the younger queen, Gagan Singh, was shot dead. The angry queen plotted with the help of Jang Bahadur and his brothers to massacre all the *bhardars*, the ruling elite of the country. On the queen's call they unsuspectingly came to a chamber, and Jang Bahadur, hidden behind the chamber's entrance, massacred all of them one by one. Dozens of senior citizens of the country were butchered. After this incidence, Jang Bahadur and his family came to be known as Ranas. He replaced the King from the centre of power, though the king remained the nominal head. Well settled in power, Jang Bahadur obtained Lal Mohar (royal order) from the King Surendra Bikram Shah, granting him the title of Maharaja Teen Sarkar on 5th May, 1849 and the rulership of Kashki and Lumjung which would pass on as hereditary privilege to his descendants. He then started calling himself Teen Sarkar. Lal Mohar was sent to the then British Governor General of India as a token of recognition of the Rana position.

The Kot massacre of the *bhardars* brought enough land under the Rana jurisdiction. To gain favour of the Brahmins and to create an atmosphere of goodwill, Jang Bahadur announced that the Birta and the Guthi lands would be returned to their rightful owners, though it was really difficult to locate the real owners almost thirty years after the confiscation. Nonetheless, most of the Guthi land was returned. Some land went also to the influential Brahmin families. The prime land in the Kathmandu valley and the Tarai region, however, remained with the Ranas. During the time of Prithvi Narayan Shah, land was given to the deserving persons for their services rendered to the crown. Under the Ranas, land came as a matter of privilege. Herein lies the difference. The highly centralised administration and prevalence of feudal system in the land prevented the emergence of a free peasantry and gave rise to slavery which continued in Nepal until 1922. It was only in 1923 that, due mainly to the insistence of the British Government of India, 60,000 people were freed from their bondage at a cost of Rs. 37 lakhs. This money, however, was made available not by the treasury but by confiscating the riches of the Pasupati Nath temple. Another equally bad practice which was prevalent mostly in the Tarai region was bondage whereby a person voluntarily agreed to lose his freedom by mortgaging himself. But once mortgaged, it was virtually impossible for him to buy back his freedom.

The Ranas endeavoured to keep all the privileges within their kith and kin and other relations, including whatever money could buy. The only other class which flourished under them were petty merchants. The growth of the middle class in Nepal came about only after the end of the Rana rule when the democratic process was set in. During the later years of the Rana rule, even the children of the trusted vassals were looked upon as prospective suspects working to bring about a change in the system. Throughout Nepal, the regime kept continuous vigil for any sign of unrest irrespective of who belonged to which class. In order to preserve the Rana rule, education was discouraged. It is not surprising that just two years before the end of the Rana rule in 1948, *Gurkhapatra*, a government owned newspaper, reported that the total number of persons holding university degree in Nepal at the time were not more than 55, out of which only 7 had a master's degree.[9]

The seeds of discontent against the regime often grew among the fast expanding families of the Ranas themselves. Even during the reign of Jang Bahadur, a plot to assassinate the mighty Prime Minsister was hatched by his own brother, Badri Narsingh, known as Bhandrkhal Parba. This dastardly act cost Badri Narsingh heavily. He forfeited his right for succession. Jang Bahadur's rolls of succession provided for the eldest among the living brothers to succeed as Prime Minister. It had many flaws. The worst was that it gave an opportunity to different but related families to plot against each other in order to gain maximum advantage on path to succession. Each prime minister would indulge in intrigues to put his own legitimate or illegitimate sons on the rolls depriving his nephews and cousins from it. This flaw in succession rolls ultimately brought about the collapse of Rana edifice by its own weight and paved the way for democratic change. Expanding Rana clan aspiring to become the Teen Sarkar became so large that the then Prime Minister, Candra Shumsher, devised a way out in 1916. According to his precept, the Rana clan was divided into three categories. Class A Ranas, being the legitimate sons, class B Ranas, who could be legitimised by the Prime Minster and be nominated to become the Prime Minister and the C class, comprising the illegitimate group, who were barred from the Prime Minister's rolls. It was natural for the Ranas belonging to class C to play a role in bringing about the downfall of Rana regime. Many class C Ranas took refuge in India in order to avoid humiliation and to cover up their social degradation. These rich Rana emigres later helped the revolutionary movement against the ruling Ranas by providing financial and emotional support.

Girls belonging to Rana families were usually married in the princely families in India. Thus even lower grade Ranas could try to upgrade their social status by having family connections with the ruling elites in India. The closed door policy pursued by the Ranas could therefore not be very effective for there was a continuous outflow and inflow between India and Nepal.

Jang Bahadur Rana, within two years of assuming full powers, had came to India with a big contingent of Gurkha soldiers to help the British to crush the Indian Mutiny of 1857. This naturally entitled him to a reward from the British rulers. Later, on his visit to England in 1908, Jang Badadur was decorated by Queen Vctoria as a 'Loyal Vassal King'.

Before the entry of the Ranas as effective rulers, prior to 1846, the concept of monarchy was not sacrosanct. There had been cases when the populace of Kathmandu had revolted and even assassinated a ruling monarch. Jang Bahadur himself deposed King Rajendra Vikram Shah with ease and crowned Surendra Vikram Shah as the monarch. In fact, Jang Bahadur could not end the Shah dynasty and usurp the crown for himself because of the British pressure. British Resident, Brian Hodson (1833-43) who laid down the general line of British policy for Nepal had written to Charles Metcalfe on the 15th July 1837 :

> We ought, if need be, to insist on effectual access to the legitimate head of state, who has for many reasons by far the greatest interest in peace and quiet. All others, scrambling for the distinction and advancement, must gain them by and through the army, which is the beginning, the middle, the end.[10]

Once this general line was laid down, the British policy did not change even after Jang Bahadur proved his loyalty to the British Queen. Jang Bahadur and his successors chose the next best thing that they could do under the circumstances. They usurped the powers of the monarch by forcibly extracting the *firman* (order) from the ruling King. To legitimise the eclipse of the monarch, a variety of divine myths were contrived and given currency.

To a certain extent the Rana despotism depended upon the support of the British rulers of India. In the British eyes, the old Rana system represented the true "tradition of Indian rule and Indian ritual.[11] Ranadom would not otherwise have collapsed soon after the British left the Indian soil.

The British had recognised Nepal's formal independence in 1923 and agreed to send her arms and warfare materials as "may be required or desired to strengthen the welfare of Nepal." Jang Bahadur had come to realise that he had to humour the British to remain in power. He did it quite successfully. The British were happy to find an ally.

REFERENCES

1. B.P. Koirala, *Democracy Indispensable for Development*, p. 31.
2. *Gorkhapatra*, 53, 3 Oct. 1951, p. 1.
3. Manifesto Adopted at the Sixth National Convention of the Nepali Congress, Birganj, Jan. 1956, p. 7.
4. *Ibid.*
5. Text of the Agreement between B.P. Koirala and Matrika Prasad Koirala reached at Calcutta, 8 April, 1952 through the mediation of Jai Prakash Narayan. *The Statesman*, (6 Aug. 1952). When asked to throw some light

on Regmi's residential election K.P. Bhattrai, Honourable speaker of the Pratinidhi Sabha had this to day, "I was General Secretary then. I knew both M.P. Koirala and Regmi. During Satyagraha period we made M.P. Koirala, as you know, President. He indeed said that he would remain so but would resign when the movement was ended. None would have liked his leadership. But we were all young then and we felt that M.P. Koirala with his maturity could guide us. But he proved both inefficient and coward. When we were to meet in Banaras (16 July, 1949) MP sent me two letters from Jogbani. First was a formal letter saying that now as the movement was suspended, he would resign. In the second — a private letter — he asked me to re-elect him as president. I was very angry at this double dealing. Some of his members supported his candidature and then I read out his formal letter. I had also written to Regmi, and we all thought that Regmi would be a better person than MP. The executive then decided to elect Regmi as President. But we soon found out that he was a greater coward, more inefficient than even M.P. Koirala. Myself and Ganeshman were instrumental in making him the president and for that we both repented very much. Then Ganeshman wrote that nasty letter to Kamaskar, which Devkota has published in his book. Anyway, when BP came outside there was no point in keeping a worthless man like Regmi, so we had to let him out."

6. *The Times of India*, 25 September, 1953.
7. For further information see, Anirudha Gupta, *Politics in Nepal*, Allied Publishers Pvt. Ltd., 1964.
8. See Levi, Sylvian Le Nepal, (type written translation with Indian Council of World Affairs Library, New Delhi.
9. *Gurakhapatra*, 48 Asadh 12, 2005 VS 8.
10. (W.W. Hunter, *Life of Brain Hodson*, London, 1896, p. 157. See Article 5 of the Treaty between Great Britain and Nepal, 1923.
11. Percival London, 1934, p. 239.

5

A BRUSH WITH DEMOCRACY

The Congress Party was invited in 1954 to join the government. Admist chaos and confusion, the movement for democracy and an elected government in Nepal was kept alive by BP and his Congress Party. After the formation of the National Cabinet on the 2nd March 1954, BP in his memorandum to king Tribhuvan wrote :

> I beg to inform your Majesty that our working committee that concluded its deliberation today has decided not to join the recently expanded cabinet on the present basis. The working committee gave a very serious consideration to your Majesty's offer of two seats in the recently expanded cabinet. In the absence of a common programme this cabinet of divergent pulls and conflicting interests lacks unity of purpose, on account of which, we feel, it cannot function effectively. It lacks cohesion. Moreover, the manner in which it was brought into being in utter disregard of the previous commitments is also indicative of an obnoxious trend in our politics to which, we feel in all conscience, we cannot subscribe.

> Apart from these considerations, the summary curtailment of the powers of Supreme Court just on the eve of the formation of the new government makes mockery of its popular basis. This retrograde action takes away the prestige of the government particularly because this step was taken only three days before the new government was installed, and if the new cabinet was of no consequence in respect of major decisions, where was the need to install it?

> In view of these considerations the working committee feels

that the Congress can serve the country better by disassociating with the present government and functioning as responsible opposition in the country."[1]

MAHENDRA TAKES OVER

Petty interest played significant role for almost five years in the politics of Nepal. In the midst of this chaos, the King vested all royal power to the Crown Prince on the 18th February 1955 and left for his treatment abroad. On 2nd May 1956, Crown Prince Mahendra was coronated and proclaimed as the King. The Crown Prince with full royal authority boldly stated:

> It has been almost four years since the inception of democracy in our country. But we have to search and research to find even four achievements to our credit in the meanwhile. It is really a matter of great pity. Should we say that democracy is in a state of infancy? Evil propensities like selfishness, greed and envy are very much noticeable in it, which are unnatural for an infant.[2]

On 16th March 1957, King Mahendra appointed a Commission consisting of five members to draft a constitution. This Commission presented to him what he had worked for. In the preamble to the Draft Constitution, it was stated that "sovereignty continues to reside in the king". A happy King Mahendra declared, "It was designed to promote the welfare of this generation and also those to come and deemed suitable for this ancient land of ours."[3] Contrary to this, the Nepali Congress had worked and hoped for people's sovereignty. But the Nepali Congress quietly accepted the Constitution. This turned out to be its gravest mistake with serious repercussions in the long run. "The gains of the revolution were heavily reaped by the crown. By this very process they managed to strifle the spirit of progress."[4] BP embossed by peoples power and King Mahendra by his own power, the tussel ensued. Both were insufflated. If they had combined their efforts, Nepal would have been a different country today.

THE DEMOCRATIC FRONT FORMED

As a reaction to the proposed Constitution, the Rastriya Congress and Prajaparisad joined hands to form a democratic front. The agreement of 9th August 1957 read as follows:

We the signatory parties who believe in the principle that sovereignty resides with the people, having felt the need for forging unity.

These parties aimed at different objectives in the elections; i.e., the Nepal Prajaparisad advocating elections for a sovereign parliament, and the rest, the Nepali Congress and the Nepal Rastriya Congress believed in having the elections for a sovereign constituent assembly. They said :

And further keeping in view the crisis that ensued from the royal palace, we have come to the conclusion that in the absence of a strong organization of the democrats, neither a sovereign parliament according to the demands of the Nepal Praja Parishad nor a sovereign constituent assembly as demanded by the Nepali Congress and the Nepali Rastriya Congress can be fulfilled.

And, as there is a possibility that the very fundamental right which the people have won after the revolution will be ended, we have decided (1) to join democratic forces and to meet the impending threat to democracy and (2) to safeguard the fundamental rights of the people.[5]

GENERAL ELECTIONS ANNOUNCED

King Mahendra announced February 18, 1959 as the date for the country's first general elections. The measure of the popularity of the Nepali Congress became clear when more than six lakh of the total electorate voted it to power with more than three-fourths of the total number of seats of Pratinidhi Sabha going to the party. For the first time, the ruling party, instead of merely talking, made attempts to implement a number of urgent reforms. On May 7th 1960, B.P. Koirala in his presidential address said.

As the Nepali Congress is a completely democratic organisation, its leadership is not vested in any particular individual but in the entire delegation of representatives. The principle of collective leadership confers its speciality and importance to a democratic set up, or we can say that in this set up the majority opinion is in itself the principle and idea of collective responsibility. I have ever derived self-confidence as well as courage, inspiration and encouragement from these elementary principles of democracy.

He further said, "while such big or small activities in the transition stage during the post-revolution period might not appear to possess much significance, it must be admitted that such seemingly small but subtle works possess an immeasurable and permanent importance in the task of strengthening the basis of democracy. It would not be an exaggeration to proclaim the truth that if the Nepali Congress had not stood four square on the side of democracy during the transition period, our general elections and the consequent hopeful situation arising therefrom would not have been possible."

On the eve of the short interlude with the democratic aspirations, the Royal family of Nepal formed a formidable party "Gorkha Parishad" of the vested landed interests along with the Ranas. They continued to occupy key positions in the administration. Army too remained in their hands. While the King had assumed powers as the supreme commander in 1951, the commanding positions in the army remained in the hands of Rana officers. The Royal and ruling families wanted to preserve these powers to themselves through the political party they had formed.

On the other hand, the hold of the Royalty, the Ranas, the zamindars and Birta owners was viewed by the democratic forces as a dead weight on Nepal's predominantly agricultural economy with hardly any industry to back it up. The democrats felt there was a need to develop small scale and cottage industries to provide conditions for a balanced growth. In fact, they wanted to implant Gandhian economic and social philosophy on the Nepalese soil. BP had inherited from Gandhiji the techniques of Satyagraha and the socialist principle of class struggle. Instead of mass production, Gandhiji had ordained production by masses on small scale and in a decentralised framework. BP knew that he had to follow Gandhiji's ideals if he wanted to wipe the tears from the eyes of every poor Nepali. He said, "My machinery will be of the most elementary type, which I can put in the homes of millions". He advocated socio-economic upliftment of the poor strata of the Nepalese society. It was his belief that, "at the core of every problem facing the country lies poverty which gets aggravated by lack of productive occupation which again can be traced back to the social injustice and increasing pressure of population". The socialist ideals of mass participation and decentralisation of power so as to bring about dynamism in the local units and to work for an integrated planned welfare of the society was a dream of BP which he strived unsuccessfully to convert into a reality in his lifetime.

The election manifesto of the Nepali Congress, for general elections of May 27, 1959, had given the party programme of establishing socialism through progressive elimination of feudal relations on land and rapid industrialization.

Besides, it promised to bring about greater efficiency in administration, eradication of all kinds of corruption and bribery, and decentralisation of powers. While accepting Nepali as the national language it stressed the need for encouraging the development of the regional languages. It guaranteed complete religious freedom with the pledge that the services of the Nepali Congress would always be there to protect the religious beliefs and practices of the people.

In respect of foreign policy, the manifesto upheld the policy of non-alignment with military camps and work for peace through the medium of the United Nations. BP Koirala's government showed remarkable sense of realism and maturity by refusing to take side on the Sino-Indian border dispute. It also laid the basis for an amicable settlement and demarcation of Sino-Nepalese border which King Mahendra later formalised.

During its short tenure the Nepali Congress government tried to introduce a number of radical legislative measures, including the bill to abolish Birta land and introduction of a taxation system on higher incomes. The introduction of the parliamentary rule in Nepal also led to certain changes in the organizational set up of the Nepali Congress. Greater emphasis was laid on building up the organization from below, starting from parliamentary constituencies and through regular constructive activities in the villages. For the first time in Nepal, remote villages were gradually being awakened politically.

At a time when lethargy of centuries was being shaken up and common people began looking up for change in and around their life, came the rude shock on 15th December, 1960, when King Mahendra suddenly dismissed the elected government and dissolved the parliament. Among a good section of the people of Nepal, the feeling was that King Mahendra feared that the popularly elected government was gaining ground among the common people and that parliamentary system was gaining strength and once this process consolidated it would eventually mean restrictions on his own arbitrary powers. And therefore he imposed his direct rule before it was too late.

King Mahendra, as Crown Prince, had seen his father languish in the palace-prison for years together, where there was always a threat to his life lurking behind. There was always a kind of subdued hostility between King Tribhuvan and the Crown Prince. Many a time BP had to intervene to diffuse the tension between them.[7]

However, no effective measure to end the medieval forms of land ownership or to channelize the economy towards progressive amelioration of the toiling peasantry could be undertaken by the new government. The efforts of any party or group to do so met with resistance from the vested interests and, in the ensuing conflict, the King never sided with the reformers. This, to an extent, has been the tragedy of Nepal. The political domination of the Ranas had ended, but their hold on Nepal's economy in alignment with the zamindars and Birta owners continued. The democratic forces, on the other hand, failed to put up a unified resistance against these feudal forces. It will not be wrong to say that the revolutionaries could hardly ever realize the strength of the reactionary forces. They failed to understand the role and character of the monarchy as well. It escaped their notice that the King's participation in the revolution was forced on him by the circumstances and that, sooner or later, his progressive role was bound to recede. The leaders had always thought of fighting the feudal forces but in reality they never fought. The untimely death of King Tribhuvan was also a set-back.

Due to these inherent weaknesses, the democratic forces in Nepal could not become strong. And many of the Nepali politicians and parties succumbed to the pressure of the vested interests. Their constant intrigues and personal squabbles would not permit the popular forces to become effective and get united against their enemies. The steps taken by Koirala government to abolish Birta land and its policy of land reform annoyed the reactionaries in Nepal, who were perpetually insinuating the King to do away with the popular government. King Mahendra who was not a democrat wanted to establish his own authority and got the opportunity that he was looking for. He dismissed the elected government on December 15, 1960, imposed his own direct rule, and called for a partyless Panchayat System. The Nepali Congress till then had not gained the status of a dominant national party. It had brought a revolution in Nepal. But it had never been a cadre based party. Its political activists joined and deserted the party at their own convenience. At the King's call, more than half of the party activists crossed over to the King's side to make a success of the partyless Panchayat system. These included some of the high ranking leaders of the Nepali Congress.

BP was badly disappointed by the dismissal of the Government. He had been throughout apprehensive of the destructive forces working against national reconstruction. He had expressed his apprehensions in his presidential address:

It is indeed a difficult task to exhort people who are undergoing a life of heart rending privations to work harder. This task had been more difficult by the destructive efforts of those elements who could not tie themselves up with the welfare of the country. When one looks at the situation from this angle one can realise the special significance of the provisions relating to kingly powers in the constitution. As the constitution is the medium which can align this force to the side of development of the country in our present state, the constitution has great utility. The country needs the co-operation of all national forces in the task of reconstruction and development. Fellow members of the Nepali Congress must be able to obtain the co-operation of these national forces by their efficiency and integrity. The forces arrayed against Nepali Congress can chiefly be divided into two classes: First, those feudal elements which are still carrying on a defeated war. It cannot be said that they might not be guilty of undesirable activities in their despair at defeat and in the frenzy of a desire for revenge. Actually, it is these elements which are responsible for the encouragement afforded to most of the provocative and destructive activities that can be seen in the country today. They are greatly excited over the abolition of Birtas, the proposed land reforms, the protection of the rights of the peasants, the progressive tax levied on land etc. and the fixation of land ceiling and the proposal for the abolition of the Zamindari system etc. Such matters are being done or contemplated in the country which have raised unextinguishable and terrible fires of anger and revenge among the feudals. This group is trying to utilise the help of organisations repudiated by the people in our elections in its clumsy attempts to prolong its own existence.

There are certain similar anti-national elements also which by means of extreme slogans and destructive activities in the midst of our uncertainties arising out of our present transition period make more complicated our problems of development.

He further cautioned: "The Nepali Congress must try to bind all other national forces into a single strand by means of which the problems of present day revolution may be solved, and the country may proceed on its appointed path for economic development and national reconstruction."

While replying to a question about the difficulties on the way of building up parliamentary democracy in Nepal, BP said: "The first difficulty we face is that of a learner. We have suffered a century of autocratic rule and there was no popular institution worth the name. The problem therefore, is a psychological one that of adjusting to the democratic ways now being introduced in the country.

Our second difficulty is administrative. Formerly, the Rana Prime Minister's word was law in the country and his orders were implemented unhesitatingly. But the situation today is different since Prime Minister cannot do anything without consulting other departments... The Congress therefore cannot work quickly, but the people are not going to be satisfied with such excuses. They sure would judge our work in relation to what we can perform in the coming five years.

In view of our limited resources and backward social economy I also think that for a few years we must give up socialism. Our first problem is the utilization of all our available resources of the country in a planned way. We must do everything to build up our capital forming capacity".

BP had been quite consistent from the beginning. Way back in 1950 during the merger of the Nepali Congress and Nepal Democratic Congress he had said:

Political democracy, however vital in the present context, is just a means to an end, a means in which although, a part of the aim is already achieved. We want political freedom because we want to build up a society after our heart, a society in which the citizens are not exploited, where there is no poverty, no in-equality, where education is free and human personality is not stunted from wants. As a matter of fact, really free society cannot exist in the midst of poverty. Eradication of poverty will be the first concern of the future Government of Nepal.

Are we prepared for this noble task of reconstruction. Are we prepared for the task of destruction, at the first instance? If we are, then let us join hands and march ahead. Tomorrow is ours. With this faith in ourselves we have combined and invite others to join us. At this time it seems mighty action, which destiny calls us to launch into. Let us not sulk in the corner nursing petty grievances, peevishly calling the fate to witness the grand spectacle of a nation marching forward and forward in a frenzy of action which has left our small selves behind, far behind. I appeal to all those who place country above everything else to join with us to achieve freedom, both political and economical.[8]

After all, we have to compress a whole stage of capitalist

growth within a decade or so. During this interim period we shall encourage everyone who has the desire to help us.[9]

SET-BACK TO DEMOCRACY

An overview of the political scenario of that time makes it clear that Nepali Congress and its leadership could not rise to the occasion to face the problem-ridden situation. BP was aware of this fact but could do nothing while the opportunity was still there. From its very inception, Nepali Congress once in a while demonstrated its revolutionary zeal, but was never able to sustain it for long. A practical leader would have first reorganised the party from the grassroots level and worked for a disciplined, ideologically oriented cadre-based party. The idealism in BP almost blunted his ability to anticipate the ruthlessness of a reinstated monarchy. He was a man who had never hankered for power. Way back in 1958 during the concluding session of Nepali Congress Mahasamiti, he had offered not to contest in the First General Elections so as to enable him to devote his energies to work for the good of the people and the country. What could be the reason behind this kind of disorientation? One answer probably could be his awareness that he was suffering from a dreadful disease which could prove fatal any moment. This awareness naturally developed in him an ability to disassociate himself from immediate issues and take a detached view of mundane problems of life. In a lesser mortal, the mere thought of cancer could have had devastating effects. BP's tremendous will power was, in a way, his personal strength. It is this inner strength that is reflected when he says, "You see I don't have long to live, three or four years at the most. If I can do something about restoring the process of democracy, may be that would be something to remember me by... The Hindu practice is to throw the ashes into water, no monuments, no tombstones. I think that is a very good idea..."

The pursuit of higher values had become an obsession for him. In simple words, he articulates his philosophy towards God and man. "First of all, nobody has defined for men what he means by God. But that part of existence in which man starts composing poems, when he is filled with that oceanic feeling, when he sees the vastness of the universe, when he sees its beauty, the flowers, that is the experience of God, or divinity. Man does not live for bread alone. There are other aspects of life which are important, perhaps more important. Those aspects are unexplained mysteries of life. If you are not aware of the mysteries, not awed by them you have not lived fully."

Sailendra Kumar Upadhyay, the seniormost member of the Rastriya Panchayat, had this to say about BP: "I have known almost all the leaders of Nepal of those days. Dilli Raman Regmi, I worked with him for a number of years. Tanka Prasad Acharya was the president of the United Front, I was its secretary. K.I. Singh I knew closely, Surya Prasad Upadhyay, Ram Hari Sharma etc. BP had a charisma and hold in the heart of his people. He was surrounded by many midgets. While BP always thought he had to rise above the level of being a leader of a nation, he had an egalitarian attitude... Every meeting with BP used to give me a feeling of fulfilment. He was a towering intellectual, could talk for hours on philosophy, poetry, women and sex. He had a beautiful way of explaining. I would go to him with my own doubts, sometimes determined to defend myself. Unknowingly he would be piercing the walls I had managed to erect around and give a simple explanation of a difficult problem".

Another set-back to the democratic movement in Nepal had come from its power hungry leaders. King Mahendra feared BP most for he knew he was uncorruptible. On May 27, 1959, BP had to be invited by the King to form the first elected government as the leader of the Nepali Congress, the majority party in the Pratinidhi Sabha. The King knew the inherent weakness of some of the leaders of Nepali Congress. Some power hungry leaders could be bought over. King Mahendra started baiting them first. For, middle and lower level workers could be bought, harassed or ignored. As soon as he had ascended the throne, he had shown unusual interest in actual governance of the country. This was the reason for continuous clash between him and the leaders. He encouraged lobbies and groups that would be loyal to him. Even as the Crown Prince, Mahendra had always been looking for an opportunity to forge strong links with the Ranas. The Ranas too saw in him as the means through which they could retain power. Earlier they had even advised King Tribhuvan to abdicate in favour of the Crown Prince. It was indeed a sad day in the history of the democratic movement in Nepal that King Tribhuvan died before the process of democratisation had really begun in Nepal. King Mahendra believed that once Koirala ministry consolidated its position, his own power will gradually wane away. A past-master in palace intrigues, the King outmaneouvered BP. BP was no match for the intriguer and the King walked over without any qualm.

Besides, BP's difference of opinion with the King on various matters kept him in constant clash with the latter. One of the major points of difference between BP and the King was over raising resources for development of Nepal. BP was of the opinion that the resources had to be mobilised from within the country by taxation and other means. He was not averse to seeking foreign aid. At the same time, he was aware that, "foreign aid in our situation, instead of helping the process of development, only creates a new class of people whose affluence is unrelated to the general economic condition of the nation as a whole". The King argued since Nepal was already getting foreign aid, it could mobilise more in the years to come, given its strategic position and other attractions.

King Mahendra believed that through foreign aid, economic development of the country could be divorced from the political process and under his authoritarian leadership pace of development could be accelerated. Subsequent history proved him wrong. Nepal even today is bracketed with the least developed countries of the world, being 8th from the bottom upward in real per capita income, having lowest literacy rates for males (39 per cent) and females (12 per cent) in South Asia. The King failed to realise that people's own effort and participation in the process of development were key elements for a successful development.

BP had a different vision, drawn from his idealism and democratic socialism. He has expressd it as follows: "Man has infinite facets. It is not only his economic aspects that define man. As a matter of fact, I feel that history's revolutions have not been inspired by the urges of belly. People don't make sacrifices unless they are enthused by some higher objectives. Consider the great Bengal famine during the war. Millions of people died in Calcutta streets but there was no revolution because their hunger was not linked with higher objectives. Secondly, I think there are two basic contradictions in man, between his anarchic elements and his social elements. The leadership is always anarchic not accepting any restraint on its freedom. The best socialist or communist society is supposed to be that of the bees or ants, but they do not evolve because there is no rebellion there. In human society anybody who wants to strike new roots is violently rejected, e.g., Christ, Socrates, Gandhi. The only comparable man who died peacefully was Budha. But what is rejected today becomes chaster tomorrow. I have tried to fulfill my anarchic, my rebellious instincts through writing novels etc., and my social instincts I have tried to fulfill through my work in politics, by trying to improve the lot of the people around me. As a socialist, I am searching for better laws to bind the people, as a writer I am breaking laws". BP all through his life had faith in Nepal's future and the strand of socialism that would suit it best. He believed in 'democracy at the political level and economic development that does justice to the masses; ... economic development to eradicate poverty otherwise political liberty would be a myth. It is not a question of idealism or putting faith in higher values of life. It is a matter of survival". BP, a high strung idealist all through his life, suffered from a kind of dilemma and tension within himself. He explains it beautifully when he says, "there is a tension in me, I feel I am an outsider in politics, my profession should have been literary pursuits. When I start writing I feel I am wasting my time".

The dilemma brings out the best personal qualities of the man. He was a great lover of all kinds of beauty, be it in nature or in his fellow human beings. He worked relentlessly to bring happiness and joy in the life of the downtrodden. He embodied courage, conviction and an innate compulsion to place the interest of his country before his own. He said time and again, "I have great ambition for my country... when some of our partymen complain that the pace is very slow, I tell them that there is no alternative to this or to that mandate. We have given ourselves that there must be national unity and national unity cannot be achieved in vacuum, which means that the peoples factor and the monarchy must combine: that there must be total understanding between these two elements of national life. The alternative to this is ruin. That is what I feel and therefore I do not contemplate any alternative to this". But he did not compromise with the King on the question of foreign aid.

BP's optimism kept the hopes about democracy alive. The set-backs in life or political career never dampened his youthful spirits. A trained revolutionary and socialist to the core as he was, the writer in him always brought out the best and noble in him. Rarely he had a feeling that he was trying to break his head against a wall. In all kinds of odd situations he would find a ray of hope. Heavy dark cloud would have a silver lining for him though he had apprehensions about democracy's survival in Nepal. In his opinion, "Nepal had to learn a whole process of democratic development rather in a short span of time. Therefore, it is imperative that Nepalese people display a great deal of caution and understanding and not get swayed by minor debacles".

The restoration of kingship in 1951 and subsequent developments in Nepal were in fact without the larger participation of the people. That precisely was the reason why BP stressed time and again that "for a democracy to survive it was important to involve the people. Lack of contact between the people and politicians could create difficult conditions for democracy to survive. The example of Pakistan was there to see, for the third world countries, who were striving to set up democratic process in their respective countries". Further, "to be able to build up a democratically robust Nation, the sanctions had primarily to come from the people and therefore their leaders had to put all their efforts at mass awakening".[10] BP, as mentioned earlier, had great respect for the last Rana Prime Minister of Nepal, Mohan Shumsher. At the time they formed a coalition government both would sit and chat together. BP relates one intimate conversation between him and the PM: The Prime Minister asked him, "Well now that you are a Minister, what is your ambition? What do you want to do?" BP said he had only one ambition: "I belonged to a lower middle class family. But I got two square meals a day, I had a small farm which gave me my basic requirements, I had few cows, I had my children studying in school here... I need 15 years to put the poorest family to the same economic satus as mine, I would retire after that." It was this kind of affection for his people that be it a local doctor, *hakim* or *vaidya* in some far-flung areas or the Director of Tata Cancer Research Institute his medical bills were paid without his family's knowledge.

BP had a clear vision of Nepal's future. He visualised a political democracy in which "monarchy... will indeed continue, but it will be adjusted to the requirements of democracy as in the United Kingdom". The monarch in Nepal, however, was not prepared to play a second fiddle. A clash between the democratically elected Prime Minister and the King became inevitable and the King emerged victorious. The coup enacted by King Mahendra, incidentally, was not against BP personally. King's enemy was the democratic system, and BP headed it. The process of democratisation was rapidly changing the socio-economic life of the Nepalese people. But King Mahendra's alibi for the takeover was that "the very existence of the country was endangered and the omens of a fratricidal civil war among the Nepalese people became visible in the horizon."[11]

In fact, rather than "the existence of the country" it was King Mahendra's throne that was at stake as perceived by him. The architect of the Congress manifesto of 1956, BP had made it clear that while they stood for the achievement of socialism in Nepal by peaceful means, monarchy would continue, but it would be adjusted to the requirements of democracy. The agenda, however, included reorganisation of agriculture on socialist lines by means of legislation and persuasion, and state planning of agriculture and industrial ventures. Such goals were naturally not palatable to the landed aristocracy, headed by the King. So the King had to act and he acted swiftly.

King Tribhuvan had cautioned BP about his son, Crown Prince Mahendra. BP should have taken measures to contain the monarchy. Since he was not unduly apprehensive on that score, it cost him many years of his life and that of the country and its people. In his enthusiasm for fair play, he missed a golden opportunity to bring the poorest family economically at par with his own. He should have kept the palace within bounds. There was nothing new in the way in which King Mahendra moved with dramatic suddeness and the general round-up which followed. His predecessors, the Ranas, used to behave exactly in the same manner. Now that the old royalty had started rallying around the King, it was but natural for him to behave that way.

The high ethical and moral standards set up by BP are well reflected in his assertion that "We have never killed any man because killing is not our policy. We are not terrorists. We did not kill a single individual. We wanted to have open encounters to start an insurrectionary movements. That was my strategy."

It is not that BP was totally ignorant about the impending coup. Kathmandu's air was thick with rumours those days. BP did nothing about it. Why was it so? While explaining his position he said, "If we ran away, he (Mahendra) will have another alibi. We had, therefore, got to be where we are and face the consequences. If I had run away — I could have done that — then the king would have said that the country was without a Government and Prime Minister has run away."

Addressing the closed door convention of Nepali Congress leaders and workers on January 25, 1961, Suvarna Shumsher, the Deputy Prime Minister in the previous Koirala Government had said, "that the people of Nepal should not rest without re-establishing democracy".

The convention later passed a resolution stating that "The Prime Minister B.P. Koirala, created an extraordinary impression in his contacts with the outside world. Wherever he went, he conducted himself in such a manner that the prestige of the country rose. It is a shame and disgrace that the Prime Minister and his devoted colleagues, who did so much for their country, should find themselves behind bars at a time when their services are most needed by the country."[12]

Although within four months of the takeover some of the veteran comrades, who had fought to overthrow the Rana regime and were in BP's cabinet and those held high positions in the Nepali Congress, joined the opposite camp. Vishwa-bandhu Thapa, a minister and Chief whip in the Parliament and General Secretary of the Nepali Congress, publicly charged,

"Koirala ministry was moving left", and, "democracy was safe in king's hand."[13]

D.R. Regmi another veteran fighter and an eminent historian appealed to "the democrats all over the world to lend support to the cause of partyless Panchayat system in Nepal."[14] It is believed that King Mahendra had discussed his plan of the coup with Suvarna Shumsher Jang Bahadur Rana, another trusted friend of BP. All of them with one voice claimed that 'the King of Nepal wants to bring new awareness in the people through a system of guided democracy'.

One possible explanation for such behaviour of BP's comrades could be that they were unable to go along with BP's commitment to socialism. The other motive which soon became apparent, was expectation of personal political gains. King Mahendra, shortly after the takeover, gave the impression that within a year, under article 55 of the Constitution (under which he had assumed direct rule temporarily) he would announce a council of ministers drawn from various political parties and other non-party individuals. Many Nepali Congress leaders were willingly drawn to this bait. They deserted the party sooner or later. Anirudha Gupta, a keen observer of Nepal's political situation, noted: "Its ranks (Nepali Congress) are composed of a floating population of political activists who join or desert it according to their convenience. More than two-thirds of those who crossed over to King Mahendra's side and helped him construct the partyless Panchayat system in 1963, once belonged to the Nepali Congress. Some were trusted lieutenants of BP Koirala."[15]

Immediately after assuming power, King Mahendra, in order to demonstrate his good intentions, liquidated all the fifteen vassal states and stripped their chiefs, called Rajas, of all powers. According to the Royal enactment, "the rulers of the abolished states will retain their present titles of Raja and receive privy purses. In case of ruling families of four big states, these privileges will continue for three generations while in the case of others they will be extended to the lifetime of the present Raja."[16]

King Mahendra took all measures to paint his former Prime Minister as 'blackguard'. In an interview given to an American news agency, he had said that he had dismissed the premier Mr. B.P. Koirala because "he was planning eventual merger of Nepal into a neighbouring state".[17] Nepal Radio in its broadcast had reported 'seizure of about 1,80,000 Indian and about 11,000 Nepalese currency from his residence'. No one believed King Mahendra's charge of currruption, nepotism against BP. In the eyes of the people of Nepal, BP was incorruptible. He had time and again proved it. Be it political power or material wealth, nothing touched him.

At the political level the King started projecting the Nepali Congress as an anti-national party. The Sino-Indian war (1962) radically changed the scenario in favour of the King. From then onwards, India went out of its way to appease the Kathmandu Durbar. India's problems with China restrained her to come out in open support of the democratic forces. India could not live up to her prestigious image projected during the early fifties as a defender of democracy. India subsequently showed her indifference to political activities being carried out by the democratically oriented political refugees and other Nepalese from the Indian soil.

Immediately after BP's arrest, some of his friends and colleagues who were in India at that time started planning for his rescue from the jail. According to BP, his sister 'had contacted (my) colleagues in Calcutta and also met Jawaharlalji and they wanted to rescue me'. His colleagues felt BP could work once again to restore democracy in Nepal; better if he was with them. Around this time Patrice Lumumba, the great leader of Congo, was killed by a military clique which had carried out a similar coup there. This brought in a wave of uncertainty and fear especially to BP's immediate family. His sister rushed to New Delhi to seek Pandit Nehru's help. Pandit Nehru assured that Nepalese rulers were not as barbaric as those of Congo.

Jai Prakash Narayan said, "In many parts of Asia, democracy had suffered at the hands of some kind of dictator or the other. But in every case some justification could be found for suppression of democracy, such as extremè curruption, nepotism, failure and instability in administration etc. In Nepal, however, the situation was different. The personal prestige of Koirala was highest in Nepal and abroad, and the democratic Government seemed to be tackling bravely and successfully the grave problems inherited from centuries of reactionary Government. Koirala Government was one of the tallest in Asia". Furthermore, "the only way we can help is by expressing our moral support to the democratic forces in Nepal. I think Indian opinion has stood unanimously behind Mr. Koirala and Nepalese democracy. I have no intention to be disrespectful to the King of Nepal but I must say that his action has been devoid of all logic and wisdom. Only most obscurantist of kings could believe in the second half of the twentieth century that unlimited monarchy could have any future in the present-day world. I think history will show perhaps sooner than expected that King by his action has injured not so much democracy as monarchy itself and particularly his throne and dynasty. King Mahendra has made himself ridiculous by claiming to have taken action in defence of democracy."[18]

Ashok Mehta, Chairman of the Praja Socialist Party, presented a resolution in the Seventh Congress of the Socialist International on the situation in Nepal. It called upon the Socialist International to affirm its solidarity with the Nepali Congress party and the people of Nepal in their efforts to regain for their country the democratic way of life. The resolution said, "The Congress extends its solidarity to Nepali Congress and the people in their country".[19] At a time when China's aggressive postures made improved relations with the rulers of Nepal—a matter of great importance to India—Pandit Nehru wrote to King Mahendra a personal letter saying "a humanitarian approach demanded that Koirala, who was very ill, should be given all medical facilities and his own doctor, if necessary, should be allowed to attend him". His letter, as Panditji had anticipated, had no effect.

On hearing that BP was not well in jail, Jai Prakash Narayan went to Kathmandu and sent in an application to the King requesting permission to meet his friend in the jail. Not only was his request granted, King Mahendra also gave him an audience later. About his talks with the king, Shri Jai Prakash Narayan later said, "So far as I remember he did not produce any cogent argument against BP."[20]

Many years of imprisonment only helped to temper his character. After the royal takeover, 'Veer Visheswar', as he was lovingly called, was once again put behind bars.

A story told by BP should be narrated here to see how he was loved by the young and old alike. BP enjoyed every moment of his life, be it in prison or outside. While narrating the happiest memories of his life, he says, "I will tell you of a recent incidence. I was on tour in a village when a girl came to see me after offering at a Shiva temple, and had put on a Tika. I was very busy but she insisted on meeting me. When my friends brought her to me she said she would like to talk to me alone. When we were alone she said, she had gone to the temple to offer her life for me. She knew, I was not keeping well and would soon be going to Delhi for an operation, so this girl, not yet married and with her whole life before her was offering her life for me. I told her, "That is too big a gift for me, what return can I give you". She said, "But I will not be here to receive your gift for I will be dead". "That day I wept for sheer joy", he added. This was BP the loved one.

REFERENCES

1. Issued by Publicity Department, Nepali Congress Kathmandu, 1954.
2. Proclamations etc. Vol. 1, part II, p. 136.
3. Proclamations, Speeches & Messages, H.M. King Mahendra, B.B. Shah Deva, Vol. 1 (July 1951-Dec. 1960), Dept. of Publications, pp. 31-32.
4. Manifesto adopted by the Sixth National Convention of Nepali Congress, Birgunj, p. 6, Jan. 1956
5. *The Commoner*, 10 Aug. 1957, Announcement was made on 15th Dec. 1957.
6. Presidential Address by B.P. Koirala delivered at the Seventh Annual Session of the Nepali Congress at Kathmandu on May 7, 1960.
7. After the death of his first wife, when the Crown Prince Mahendra wanted to marry another Rana girl, King Tribhuvan is quoted to have told BP, "You don't know my son. He is a thorough reactionary. He is a diehard Rana supporter. He wants to marry a Rana girl and his reactionary attitude will be strengthened by the girl he wants to marry. The people will also not like that the King should find a bride for his son from the much-hated Rana family. So it is in the interest of democracy, in the interest of my dynasty, that he should marry another girl, a non-Rana girl". (See *Nepal's Experiment with Democracy*, Bhola Chatterjee, p. 17).

BP's reaction was typical of a liberal. He said, "This would be very cruel. How could a girl influence the King even if she comes from a Rana family?" To this the King said, "You don't know my son, he will make Nepal, he will make all of you weep." Later history of Nepal shows how right king Tribhuvan was in his assessment of his son.

8. On Unity and Thereafter, BP Koirala *Nepal Today* (Calcutta) 12-13 Issue, March-April, 1950.
9. "Decade in Doldrum, *1951-1961*," Anirudha Gupta, p. 24, unpublished monograph.
10. *The Statesman*, 9 Nov. 58.
11. Proclamation, Speeches and Messages, H.M. King Mahendra Vikram Shah Deva, Vol. II, Dec. 1960-65, p. 134.
12. *The Times of India*, 3 Jan. 1961.
13. *The Hindu*, 9 Jan. 1961.
14. *Asian Recorder*, February 19-25, 1961, p. 3812.
15. *The Times of India*, 3 Jan. 1961.
16. *The Times of India*, 11 April 1961.
17. *New York Times*, 6 Jan. 1961.
18. *The Statesman*, 13 Feb. 1961.
19. *The Hindu*, 13 Feb. 1961.
20. *The Indian Express*, 26 Oct. 1961.

6

PRISON MAKES A WRITER

A king incarcerated him; the world leaders abandoned him. King Mahendra was scared that BP would emerge as a world leader. It was evident that gradually he was getting out of Indian influence. If New Delhi could not control him how could the Palace ? BP found for himself that the interest of India, United Kingdom, United States and China converged. All had their own petty interest to fulfil so they forgot BP. When the Palace dismissed his ministry and imprisoned BP it became easy for the rest of the world to forget him. BP mused behind the prison walls.

Some men emerge from prison as heroes and martyrs whereas some others face the world as though they were already a forgotten tragedy. Eight years in jail, cut off from the rest of the world, BP searched for an identity in his solitary confinement. His own creative talent came to his rescue. He kept his peace and tranquillity and began writing about varied aspects of human affairs of conflicts, sorrow, happiness, faith and love. Most of his writings like *Narendra Dai*, *Suminma*, *Modiyain*, etc. were done in Sundari Bandigriha (jail). The triangle in love attracted him most. He wrote about it in his short novel *Narendra Dai*. Life has its tragedies. It does not mean, however, that there cannot be happiness in it. Happiness can sometimes be cruel, but sadness has a sensibility inherent in it. Otherwise unhappiness could become unbearable.

At a tender age, BP had come to India with his father who was himself a political refugee. He had a flair for writing. Early in school he had started writing in Hindi. About his early pursuits he says, "There was a highly celebrated journal edited by Munshi Prem Chand. I am very grateful to him as well as to one critic, Shantipriya Dwivedi. Prem Chand used to edit and publish a literary periodical called *Hans* from Banaras. I was a student in Banaras, where I came into contact with him and Dwivedi. I wrote a story and Prem Chand read it. I corrected it according to his instructions and he published it in the next issue of his magazine. I used to write very short stories, lyrical you might call them, which ran into one or two pages, and Prem Chand encouraged me."

BP acknowledged Munshi Prem Chand as his Guru in creative writings. He says, "Prem Chand was a very simple man. I was then a student, a Nepali student at that. I did not belong to Banaras, I was a refugee, but he was very kind to me. I was also in touch with a great Indian poet Jaya Shanker Prasad." Another person who influenced BP in the initial stages was Rai Kishan Das, who founded Bharat Kala Bhavan, later gifted it to Banaras Hindu University. BP's first story was published in *Hans*. A few other stories were published in *Vishal Bharat*, in Calcutta. No doubt this gave a tremendous boost to a young writer whose very first stories got published in the prestigious magazines of that time.

BP was fond of travelling long distances by car. His advocate friend Mr. Sagar Singh with whom BP had become quite close after his release from Nepali Jail and self-imposed exile in Varanasi narrated his experience of such car rides together. "On the way he recited his own poems or short stories looking out of the window. Once in right mood he would go on in his soft voice and envelope the whole atmosphere without raising his voice. After the tale had been told he expected his friends to take it up. He would listen to their stories or poems engrossed and later in a most unoffending manner would give his comments, which inevitably would be helpful to the author in improving his writings."

In a way, the people of Nepal and Nepali literature owe a debt to King Mahendra for confining BP in a solitary cell in Sundari Jail. All of a sudden BP had all the leisure at his disposal away from a hectic public life, to devote to writing. It provided him an opportunity, even though a forced one after a long time to reflect and write, an activity dear to him since adolescence and his creative mind began flowing unbound.

His novel, *Narendra Dai*, is a description of a complicated relationship narrated by a young boy, still unprejudiced by social norms and taboos. In the end, the reader views the issue from the eyes of the narrator and is unable to find fault in any of the characters. Each character in his own way stands justified. Their suffering leaves a lingering sadness which lasts long after one has finished reading.

That is the beauty of BP's writings. They make the reader sit and think. The last paragraph of this novel runs thus, "On the banks of river Koshi, on its sand, Narendra, Gouri and Munnariya have made a play of a triangle. Time and fate blew it up. The triangle has disappeared. Now that innocent sand dune is waiting wide eyed for the zero to appear and will wait and is still waiting."

Surya Bikram Gewali was one who first induced BP to write in Nepali. About this experience BP says, "I wrote one story in Nepali I think in the early 1930, and it was published in a prestigious paper in Kathmandu. And that came as a bombshell because in those days story writing had not developed, there being only mythological stories or symbolic stuff. My stories were psychological."

Most of BP's stories are woven around women undergoing suffering because of their aspirations. They often are in conflict with the social norms. They are striving to get over a difficult situation. As a writer it was spiritual success rather than material success. This was of prime importance to BP. BP in his deliverance of character proved to be a keen observer of human emotions.

He was likewise fascinated by the bounty and beauty of nature. In his writings both these aspects of life are integrated so beautifully as to take the writings at times to breath-taking heights. He begins *Suminma* in this vein : "From the nook and corners of the Himalayan ranges Kaushiki river, making a serpentine curve, getting released from the lap of the mountain like a naive maiden for the first time getting freed from her mother's lap roams around without any restraint, so is this river, roaming with full force in the Varaha area with thousands of hisses and screams, runs forcefully down."

To BP life has its tragedies but the happiness of being alive, seeing nature's glory at different times of days, months and seasons, the sensation generated by breeze, morning glow, rain drops, all make life worth living. Yet life is also made of conflicts. In *Suminma*, the conflict depicted is one between the two cultures. *Suminma* belongs to a period when Brahmanic rituals and practices were gradually being extended from the Gangetic plains to the mountainous regions. A conflict between the tribal value system and the new Brahmanic culture was inevitable. Somdutt, a young Brahmin ascetic and Suminma a daughter of the nature get into an argument regarding penance and violence. She tells Somdutt, "If one tries to destroy the ways of nature it only means that one is trying to destroy one's own self." (p. 24). "The hawk does not commit violence for it kills to eat. When we slaughter cow it is not violence. The hunting done by your prince for the sake of pleasure is real violence. Your religious books have praised the war of *Mahabharat*, that is real violence. Your religious books are going against the ways of the nature that is why there is an increase in violence in the world."

Somdutt in his firm and clear voice chastises illiterate Kirati girl, "this is the result of your bad upbringing. You don't even know the difference between violence and non-violence."

Somdutt, the ascetic, in spite of his efforts at restraints, gets drawn towards Suminma. One day in the heat of argument she blurts out at his duality, "In you there is a hell somewhere. It tries to peep out, again and again. By going against nature's way you are trying to build within yourself a dangerous empty pit. Nature is being thrown out from your system and in its space you are trying to fill up with good and bad deeds. By defying natural instincts you believe that you have become religious. That is wrong way of thinking." (p. 15). The story concludes thus:

A Brahmin youth who was trying to scratch nature to make his own place for living has gradually been retaken by nature. There is a saying long, long ago in Traita yuga. Sage Vishwamitra also had tried, to scratch the earth on the same spot. In the blood stream of the Kirata tribe here mingled a Brahmin blood. In the stream of blood a drop of blood hardly makes a difference. River Koshi was flowing with force and the peaceful atmosphere of nature was being pierced as usual. In the loneliness of the forest and sky, Somdutt's hut got engulfed."

BP's novel *Hitler and Yahudi* deals with ravages of the Second World War. The emotional distress suffered by David, who, in the prime of his life, healthy and good looking, has the eye of a man who has suffered and is suffering the havoc of war and the discrimination his people have suffered for centuries. The narrator has not read the history of Jews but he feels that one can see the experience of a race in the eye of its members for in some unguarded moments it quietly reflects in their eyes. In a soft voice David said, "There is a continuous opposition publicised against Israel by the Arabs in Asia." This novel was not completed in the first confinement. During his second sojourn in jail, BP took it up again, and wrote a few more pages. But his release when he was in the midst of the novel once again made it impossible to complete it. Shitij Prakasan did well to bring it out as it was left by BP for it really does justice to BP's creative achievements.

BP initiated a new trend in Nepali literature. As he said "I think in regard to the style my stories were some kind of a new experiment in Nepali literature, and I became famous immediately. I wrote a few stories, and then Surya Bikram Gewali, who was secretary of the Nepali Sahitya Sammelan, a literary organization in Darjeeling, wrote to me saying he was bringing out a collection of Nepali stories and I should write some new stories for it. I contributed three strories which the critics thought were very good. Again, Surya Bikram wanted to publish a collection of my stories and I consented. Whatever I wrote created an impact and people talked about it."

BP was influenced by great Russian writers like Pushkin, Dostovesky, Tolystoy, Turgenev, Chekhov, and Gorky. He considered Tolstoy to be the world's towering literary personality. Among the French masters he liked Anotole France, Maupassant and Hugo. In his style of writing short stories, it was Chekhov who influenced his style. It was BP who for the first time introduced Existentialism in Nepali literature and

Satre became known to the Nepalese literary circles through BP's writings. But it was Albert Camus who was his favourite. While talking about his likings he says, "I am afraid my taste in literature is rather eleatic. I did not read much after I became Prime Minister. Among authors, my favourite author was and still is Albert Camus in whose writings I get rather exhilirating ideas. There is very little original ideas in the present world of writers, but as a contrast, Camus came to me as a great surprise. Perhaps the quest for original ideas drew me to Shaw and Bertrand Russel. You will be surprised to know that I was once deeply influenced by C.E.M. Joad. Again I came across Aldous Huxley who still continues to be one of my favourite authors. Among political philosophers, Marx greatly influenced me... But I did not read his books in original. *Capital* appeared too terse and boring to me. But Engle's *Anti-Duhring* had greatest influence on me. In fact Engle's writings had greatest influence on my political philosophy."

Regarding poetry, "First of all, I like English poetry. I am very catholic in my taste. I like Shakespeare, his sonnets more than his dramas, and Marlowe. I like all the romantic poets: Keats, Shelley, Byron, but not Wordsworth to that extent. Then I like Swinburne for his music, his cadence, and I like Browning for his dramatic monologue. I like some of Tennyson's poems, particularly 'Crossing the Bar' and' John Masefield."

Among Indian writers, Rabindra Nath Tagore, Munshi Prem Chand, Sumitra Nandan Pant, Nirala and Jaya Shankar Prasad impressed him. Among the Nepali writers he was impressed by Balkrishna Sama, and Lakshmi Prasad Devkota.

In his writings, BP remained a non-conformist. There was always a thrill in looking at a problem from an entirely different angle rather than following the prevailing norms. He admired Gandhiji and believed him to be a non-conformist. "Gandhiji was a class apart, one of the greatest of all times. Not that I subscribe to all that Gandhiji prescribed, but he has been my life's genius."

He read and reread the *Gita* during his long sojourn of eight years in jail. He says, "I read all the commentaries but Gita did not satisfy me". His non-conformist tendencies hindered and Gita could not seep into his conscience.

To highlight unanswered questions in the Gita, BP wrote a novellete *Modiyain* (wife of a grocer). The hero of this novel, a young boy of seven accompanies his father's helper Misheerji and goes to Darbhanga town. The boy tells Misheerji that he wants to see the palace of the king and they went there.

After sight-seeing, Misheerji leaves the boy with Modiyain, the grocer's wife to complete his errand. The excitement of the day and the mysterious surroundings of the shop next to a big lake creates a kind of a nightmare in the mind of the boy. Twice in his sleep he screams. Modiyain, hearing the boy scream, comes, sits besides him and starts telling him the story of the great war, *Mahabharata*. In her soft voice Modiyain was saying, "like wise Krishna kept on hammering on the human weaknesses to Arjuna making him inert and humble. Krishna then recited in his soft inducive voice, eighteen chapters of Gita just before the deluge in Kurukshetra, the war of Mahabharata."

It is here that BP looks at the great war from the angle of human suffering, suffering of the woman in particular. The preparations of the war, the anguish which the womenfolk of Hastinapur suffered just before the war is beautifully depicted in the novel. Regarding the *Gita* and its narrator Krishna, the episode runs thus: "At noon we, friends assembled at Surya Kund (pond). Everyone said that Krishna was trying to mislead. He is not trying to solve the problem in a just manner. Some went on to say that Krishna was the incarnation of God. He had come to earth to reduce human burden by undertaking the war of Mahabharata. When we heard noise coming from the battle-field we shivered out of fear. In our hearts we started praying for our husbands, brothers, fathers, and uncles. God, please save them all. I was in the first bloom of my youth like a deer struck by an arrow I started staggering and praying—God please don't wipe out *sindoor* from my forehead. But the God did not listen to prayers. The preparations for war went on day after day." (*Modiyain*, p. 58). The characters involved in *Mahabharata* war are normal human beings, with all the attendent weaknesses. "It is said that the agonies of the souls of women whose near and dear ones were killed in this war have been searching for their dead bodies in vain for centuries and will be roaming around the earth for many more centuries to come till they find them. The anguish and tragedy suffered by common man, who fights in a battle which is not for him directly is greater."

After spending a day and night at Darbhanga, the boy is on his way back. In the train he again dreams all kinds of dreams. A dream voice of Modiyain repeatedly calls him from far away, from the sky: "Nane, (the little one), don't be great like the heroes of Mahabharata. Their greatness brought the holocaust of war, just be a good man..." (*Modiyain*, p. 60). BP all his life strove to be that good man.

Every human being has a dilemma peculiar to himself, because he is neither a beast nor a god. A human being is a member of the society, yet there is a non-conformist streak that propels him to defy social norms. A few of them rebel, others comply. Thus, each individual becomes different from the other.

Teen Gumti is a novel which deals precisely with the problem of a rebel woman, Indramaya. At the age of forty-five, has reached a point in life where she finds no reason to struggle anymore. As though she had carried the heavy burden far too long, she wants to put it down and rest a while:

Today she was in a reflective mood. She thought in the ocean of womanhood she too would have been one small drop, had she early in life not taken three major decisions. One, she had left everything, her family, society and friends and went alone to live with Pitamber, the man she loved, although he was a Brahmin and she a Newar. Her second decision, which she had felt unitl now as "my own decision", somehow after so many years did not seem to be right. It was the decision which destiny had forced her to take. The imprisonment of Pitamber, the loneliness which she suffered at that time seems to have forced the decision.

Today she felt, although an individual takes a decision, it is one's own fate which dictates the path. Even when Pitamber was around, she had developed a kind of an attachment for Ramesh which later re-inforced her decision to live with him. After Pitamber's imprisonment when she decided to live with Ramesh, for the first time she felt guilty although she had never felt guilty about living with Pitamber. It was much easier to take decision against the prevailing norms of the society but it was difficult to take decisions, against one's own conscience, her own *Id*.

She had always believed, the love which she had got was the only real thing but today while analysing her own self she could not distinguish whether the essence of love was her soul or her body.

Almost twenty years ago, when her husband Pitamber was in jail she had fallen for and became fond of Ramesh and concieved his child. When Ramesh came to know that she was bearing his child, his attitude changed. He started coming to her house less frequently. When her husband Pitamber came home after his jail term, he was prepared to live with Indramaya only if she gave up her daughter, Rama. For just one small fault of her mother, Rama's father was not her mother's husband. Rama had to live a life of emotional deprivation. Up till now she had grown up without a father's protection. It was only mother's love which had sustained her so far.

Indramaya had to give up society for the sake of her love. She had to give up her peace and tranquillity for the love of Ramesh, and finally when she had become a mother she had to give up her husband and all other happiness for the sake of motherhood. When Indramaya found that there was no chance of any compromise with her husband, there was only one course left. She left the house.

Later when she learnt that Pitamber was prepared to settle her daughter somewhere, the whole thing looked without any purpose to Indramaya. The issue was not the settlement of her daughter. The problem was with her womanhood and her fundamental right, women's right to be loved and her right of procreation both must be achieved together. She did not want to leave her daughter and at the same time she wanted to regain the love of her husband, each in its place as both were equally important to her. As usual she once again had to sacrifice one for the sake of the other. BP says,

"Women is never ending element in life. Man is simple but woman is complex." In our day-to-day life, prescribed social norms are so predominantly pro-male that any step which a woman takes against 'the prescribed norms, makes her branded as "complex" whereas for a man it does seem normal.

BP attached much significance to fate in day-to-day life. It becomes evident when he says, "I am in politics not as a matter of deliberate choice. I am a member of Koirala family, I grew up in politics and it was but a matter of choice that I should join it."

This feeling always preoccupied his mind as though a continuous debate was going on. He doubted his abilities as a leader. At the same time, he also knew that he could not be a writer alone. This doubt and debates lend poignance to human predicament of his character. In both his writings and politics, his sincerity paid rich dividends.

7

BP REMAINS UNDAUNTED

Sundari Jail, a camp jail, eighteen kilometres away from Kathmandu, had become a second home for BP during long years of his imprisonment. Nepal saw many ups and downs during this period. King Mahendra's royal proclamation had put BP ministry under framed up charges of misuse of power. Other charges including, "encouragement of corrupt practices [which] had led to widespread prevalence of misunderstanding and misconceptions and weakened the administrative apparatus, rendering the council of ministers wholly incapable of maintaining law and order in the country [... and] as a result of the encouragement received by the anti-social elements, a situation was developing which was apparent to all would have the effect of imperilling the national unity." In the name of preventing these malpractices and preserving the national unity, the King under his emergency powers and with the help of the army not only dismissed the popularly elected government but also was able to curb insurrectionist attempts by the junior members of the Nepali Congress following his coup.

On the day the government was dismissed, BP had gone to inaugurate the first general conference of Nepal Tarun Dal. He urged the youths to work for establishing democratic socialism. According to him, "This alone could ensure a society where man would cease to be an object of exploitation by man".[1] Nothing daunted an unjust ruler to stop him from crushing the delicate structure of democracy which was just one year seven months old. Emboldened by his success, the King introduced a New Panchayat Constitution in 1963, claiming that "parliamentary democracy was not suited to the genius of Nepali people."

Humming voices of resentment, however, continued to reach the Palace. To stop this, King Mahendra resorted to a Security Act under which everyone was presumed to be an informer. The Act provided: "It makes it incumbent upon officials, landlords, pensioners and even their parents under the threat of loss of their jobs, land and pensions, other punishments to inform against those engaged in anti-government activities." This was King Mahendra's way of building up a popular government in Nepal.

BP had no means to counteract all the misinformation and charges labelled against him by the Palace, even going to the extent of dubbing him as anti-national. He demanded an open trial by an independent judiciary so that people could judge his conduct and give a verdict. At that time, he was facing seven charges of treason, each carrying death penalty. It was a curious situation the accused himself was crying from the housetop for a trial which he was denied. Since his demand fell on deaf ears, he took recourse to his familiar weapon, Satyagraha, and went on a hunger-strike. He also demanded certain facilities for political prisoners one of which was that they should be allowed to see close relatives.

This time jail term lasted eight years, most of which was spent in solitary confinement. His struggle for democracy and weapon of Satyagraha attracted the attention of Amnesty International to take up Koirala's case during his various imprisonments and plead with the King for his release.

BP's only strength was people's faith in him, and his honesty and integrity. People refused to believe the false propoganda unleashed by the despotic king because they knew their leader well. A letter which he wrote to his wife, Shushila, from Sundari Jail has an important tale to tell about BP's character and integrity: "As I am now a plain and simple Bishwesar Prasad Koirala, whom the King does not know and no more his Prime Minister to whom he had lavished those gifts. I feel I have no right to keep them". (King Mahendra and his wife Ratna had presented a watch, a record-player and a bracelet to Koiralas). In the same letter he permitted his wife to take up some job.

A fragile man, BP had to fight relentlessly on all fronts, be it curbing Indian interference, trying to Place the palace in proper perspective, super powers, fedual elements in the country or even his own self-seeking partymen. He never lost his poise. Even after suffering the worst kind of treatment from the King, his spirit was undaunted. He said, "Because the worst that the King could do has already been done to me, so I have no apprehensions, nothing to fear from the King." On the issues of national importance, personal vendetta was of no consequence to him. He said, "I want to maintain kingship, because if we want to save our nation, if we want to build our country, even if we want to build our democratic polity, we need the assistance of the King. If we fight with the King our energy will be exhausted, in the process we shall destroy our nation as well."

When younger members in the party were toying with the idea that a mass upsurge could force an unwilling king to bestow democratic rights to his people, BP resisted it. According to him in such a situation in all probability foreign powers would infiltrate the movement and it could go out of control. In such a situation, "both the king and ourselves will get locked in a struggle in which we shall be prisoners of a strategy devised in foreign capitals."

DISCONTENT AGAINST PARTYLESS PANCHAYAT SYSTEM

In spite of all manipulations, King Mahendra could not stop the feeling of gradual disillusionment of the Nepalese people against partyless Panchayat system. Many districts in Nepal reported political unrest and rioting. Nawal Parasi district reported disturbances in 1966. The immediate cause of unrest was Government policy regarding citizenship rights. Early in 1962, in the eastern Tarai region of Janakpur, there was an unsuccessful attempt made on King Mahendra's life. In 1972 there were peasant and student unrests forcing police to open fire. This year witnessed also the suspension and detention of four members of the Rastriya Panchayat for demanding broad based elections to the Panchayat and more fundamental rights for the people. Students unrest was reported from Morang College also.

In this charged atmosphere, many of the murders, violence, arson and looting were ascribed to Naxalites, particularly in the south-eastern belt of Jhapa, Biratnagar and Jamalpur areas. In August 1972, armed Nepali Congress volunteers attacked a sub-police station in Itaripur. Singh Durbar, which housed Nepal's entire Secretariat, was set on fire. Use of grenade by the disenters was reported from different parts of the country. One was thrown at a posh hotel in Kathmandu.

The general deterioration in the law and order situation in the country prompted Subarana Shumsher, the acting President of the Nepali Congress in exile, to announce on the 15th May 1968 an offer for reconciliation, as he thought 'the forces of subversion were threatening the basic fabric of Nepalese life.' BP was released on the 30th October 1968. At this critical juncture, providence played a big role. King Mahendra died, his heir-apparent King Birendra succeeded to the throne. Nepali Congress leaders and workers were released after seven years in detention on the condition that 'they could either work within the panchayat system or settle down to non-political life.' How could a born political fighter BP take to non-political life? It was almost an insult to his ideals and beliefs. A page of his prison diary written on April 15, 1967 reads, "Democracy and fight for it are the only political issues of the world today. Democracy is indivisible." Ganesh Man Singh, at the time of his release, noted that "the release of B.P. Koirala and the pardon granted to Subarna Shumsher and his associates were the result of foreign pressure and the realization of growing danger faced by Nepal."

BP ON SELF-EXILE

BP's release provided him an opportunity to fight against the partyless Panchayat system. It was simply impossible for BP to comprehend that there could be a democratic Government without people's participation. On a self-imposed exile he once again went to India and started his political activities. Varanasi was once again his headquarters. Upper-most on his mind was to bring together once again the young and dedicated Nepali Congress activists. Again I refer to a page of his prison diary which reads : "In freedom man is made responsible for his acts. In dictatorship when freedom is denied both the ruler and the ruled are irresponsible—the former because he is unaccountable and the latter because he acts under duress." He wanted the ruler and the ruled to work freely and in a responsible manner. Though it was not difficult to build the movement anew for the second time because the ground was already prepared and the young activists were getting restless for a strong insurrectionary movement. BP was faced with the problem of finances and arms. He whole-heartedly started collecting money. All the money collected around this time was spent on buying arms. It came from unknown quarters.

DHANKUTA EPISODE

It will be worth while to mention here one small incident which took place during this time. In April 1971, a group of revolutionaries from East Pakistan (now Bangladesh) made a request to BP for arms. BP says, "Jai Prakash also told me that I should help them with arms if I had any to spare." This was the time when the Indian Government had not yet given any assurance of support to the revolutionaries of East Pakistan. Although BP had little to spare, yet a truck-load of arms was sent to East Pakistan with two young Nepali Congress activists, Chakra P. Bastola and Shushil Koirala and Colonel Rai, an instructor.

Immediately afterwards, following a rough hew a lot of discussions, decision was taken to send a consignment of arms to Okhaldhunga. Twenty-six young revolutionaries provided cover. There was a betrayal. The convoy had taken shelter inside a cave near Dhankuta because of bad weather it was snowing. Early in the morning the Royal Nepalese soldiers started throwing hand grenades inside the cave. The result was total annihilation. Most of them died on the spot, some were shot dead later. These brave sons of Nepal, who wanted to bring democracy to their country paid the price with their life. The leader of the group was Captain Thapa. Second in command was Angami Rai. Captain Thapa was shot dead later. When the news was announced on the Radio, BP was in Jaipur trying to collect another consignment of arms with his niece Shailaja

Acharya. About this incidence BP says "I knew I could as well have gone which them and be killed. Th's thought saved me from collapse.

This was a great shock and I had no more moral inclination to go on with this kind of thing. I would not say that I bade farewell to arms because of that event. But that did have an impact, it was a terrible shock to me." This was an irreparable loss.

RETURN FROM SELF-EXILE

After seven years of exile, BP decided to go back to his country. People had different speculations about the motives behind this decision. BP had this to say: "Some people feel that because Mrs. Gandhi made it difficult for us to live in India we came back to Nepal. That is a peripheral consideration." His brother Girja Prashad recalls, "While having our morning cup of tea in Varanasi he told me, I am leaving for Nepal. I was taken aback. I said "No". He started giving his reasons to which I replied: Sandaju! I can't give counter arguments to your logic but in the heart of heart, I do not like this idea."

The call for national unity given by BP brought mixed reactions. Some thought it to be a move for surrender. Others called it a clear indication to come within the folds of the King. There were many other considerations. The main issue was the imposition of emergency in India. It had pained BP so much that he told his friends, "It is better to live under your own king in Nepal than to live under the democratic queen of India." The happenings in Iran around the same time gave a clarion call to the kings of the world that absolute monarchy was a thing of the past. King Raza Pahalwi's fate, it was hoped, would teach the absolute monarch of Nepal to mend his ways. About the then prevailing political condition of Nepal BP says, "When I came from exile there was total darkness. People thought I was committing some kind of suicide. Even Ganesh Man Singh thought that the choice before us was between slow death in India and a dramatic suicide in Nepal and we had chosen the second course. BP always believed that 'Revolution is an inherent right of the people which comes under the category of fundamental rights.'

The moment their plane landed in Nepal, BP and his comrades Ganesh Man Singh, K.P. Bhattarai and others were taken under custody. During those days, he was so apprehensive of the dangerous phase of political situation in Nepal that he gave a press statement just before emplaning, "Till yesterday, our struggle was only for the democratic rights of the people. We, therefore, gave emphasis on democratic aspects. Today a new dimension has been added to it. Nepali Congress has to shoulder twofold responsibility. The second responsibility is the protection of the existence of the country. We have realised two facets in the condition of today's Nepal, nationalism and democracy both are at stake."

BP had gone to New York for his treatment, Sailendra Kumar Upadhyay the foreign minister of Nepal wanted an explanation from BP about his policy of National reconciliation to which BP replied, "Look! King has his thrown at stake and people have their liberty at stake, there is mutuality of interest. When I talk of National reconciliation, the King, as a kingpin of nationalism and democracy, has to come forward and we have to give him a chance." Then Upadhyay asked him, "What is the difference between you and me. We who joined the Panchayat knew that the country was not yet ready for democratic socialism. We thought under the aegis of the King, we will bring about this change. King had said he was not against democracy only that he wanted democratic norms to go to the masses at the grass root level. So what is the difference?"

To this BP's reply was: "There is a big difference, when you went to the King you went to him as an individual, I went to him on behalf of the masses, the organised force." He further said, "You are organised because you have the blessings of the King. Once this is withdrawn, you are finished."

"We are organised not by his blessings, we are organised because we have fought battles, we have opposed him. We are giving a chance to him, we are not surrendering."

BP ON TRIAL

No one knew where they were detained after their arrest. While under detention BP requested time and again to the authorities that he should be allowed to meet the King, which he was denied. Subsequently, the authorities arranged for a trial. The first question which BP asked the Magistrate was, "All of us are civilian prisoners, why are we being kept under military custody?" Thereafter the prisoners were kept under police surveillance.

In his defence before the court, BP said, "I have only this to state regarding the charges labelled against me : None of my activities, nor of the Nepali Congress can he termed or have been detrimental to nationalism and sovereignty of Nepal. I am a democrat and a nationalist. Such allegations as acting against nationalism and sovereignty were labelled against me even during the regime of Rana Prime Minister, Mohan Shumsher or when King Gyanendra was enthroned. The forces in power during that period had styled the opponents of their system as anti-national elements. Democratic struggle and peoples revolution were termed counter-productive and regarded as a direct attempt against national sovereignty. On these grounds charges were filed against the democrats. The same thing is happening today."

The dare devil path taken by BP and his comrades did not go unnoticed. Socialists and democrats all over the world kept following the farce of a trial. There was no choice left for the monarch. He had to show to the world that he had the interest of his country uppermost in mind. A new wave of relaxation became perceptible in Nepal. The king adopted some measures to win back the democrats of the country to his side. The steps taken included amendment of the constitution, announcement of a referendum and the introduction of adult franchise. In spite of such measures, the people of the country did not cooperate with the palace. Thus, once again the King had to fall back upon the old methods.

RECONCILIATORY APPROACH

Having sensed the dangers of chaotic political situation, BP wanted to have reconciliation with the King. The logic behind the reconciliatory posture taken by BP was explained by him as "In the situation of Nepal today we are unable to cope up with big dislocation and instability. We have to depend on peaceful method of transformation, political as well as social. We need the co-operation of the king for this. In case if we say we don't need his support then perhaps the instability and revolution which takes place will create such chaos that we may not be in a position to steer it."

The much awaited audience with the King was granted initially with reluctance and later willingly. In such meetings BP would speak of the same things over and over again, that the King should be partisan in favour of the people who wanted the King to be modern and a democrat. "I want democratisation of kingship and the King should play a role in that. As a matter of fact, I am banking on his assessment of the situation on his retaining the interests of the dynasty at heart... after all a dynastic king without a kingdom is meaningless. So he will be interested in the stability of the country. That is the rock bottom of his self-interest on which I have been harping again and again."[2] In all such meetings, BP would tell the King, "Any strategy on my part which can serve that interest of yours will serve you too". He added, "My thesis which I also maintained at my trial is that the people have an inherent right to take up arms when no other avenues are open to them to express their opposition."

KING SENDS BP ABROAD FOR TREATMENT

On one day of his trial, BP felt giddiness and loss of sight. The doctors were quite worried. He was immediately summoned by the King. King Birendra wanted to know from the doctors at what critical and dangerous stage BP's health was. After listening to them, the King advised BP to go immediately abroad for treatment. BP replied that he had no means to do so. King Birendra for once showed his generosity and asked BP to get ready for the next morning flight. Within an hour passports of BP and Sushila were ready. He was assured that his expenditure would be taken care of by the government of Nepal. BP and his wife left for United States of America for his treatment in June 1977. It was King Birendra who had taken the initiative to send him for treatment abroad saying, "Nepal needs your services for many more years to come." Royal Cabinet took the opportunity to pass a resolution praising the King for his large-heartedness, but it wanted that 'so long as BP is in Nepal he should be under detention and should leave the country as a *detainee.*' It is reported that the cabinet also insisted that BP should give in writing that he would not indulge in anti-government propaganda while he was away in foreign land. BP refused to accept this condition: he was prepared to stay back rather than accept such a condition. On the other hand, according to BP, the King had told him, "Alright if you want to be released just now you may go home from here." To this BP had replied he would first go to the prison to meet his comrades and Ganesh Man Singh and only then go home the next morning.

Analysts suggest that BP's release was due to the international pressure. President Jimmy Carter advocated human rights and total rejection of emergency measures in India by the Indian voters to some extent played a role. Whatever might be the force behind his release, BP aggressively told his mind to his audience.

In America in defiance of the wishes of the Nepalese cabinet. "I told them [American leaders] that they do the opposite of helping democrats in the third world". He said he did not want any other help from Americans except the expenditure of breath. He said, "I want words from the leaders of America that you want to see democracy in my country. Show your commitment to your own ideology of democracy. We do not want your military or financial assistance. We hope that when President Carter takes a stand on human rights, he does not mean it in cold war context but means precisely what he says. If there is a little support for our cause, it could help. Congressmen, senators, other officials — if they will just say, that they want democracy in Nepal let them write to King privately, may be or publicly and my battle is won."[3]

ON HIS RETURN

A dialogue had continued between BP and the King, even though BP was still under formal trial. BP reports, "I told him about my point of view, about the need for unity between the monarchy and democratic forces to save the country." According to BP they had three historic tasks to perform—building up of institutions, giving rights to the people, and economic development. For proper fulfilment of these tasks, the King of course, had to be dynamic, but the system too must be such that the people are motivated, are involved, and feel responsible for their country and its development and for the stability of the political system." He, later on, reported that he had emphasised three more points. "We should not permit a Sikkim type of situation to develop here. We should not allow a situation to develop as in Iran, and we should not allow a situation like that developing in Afghanistan."

BP felt that the traditional authority of the King must be utilised to solve the problems of the country. Nepal was not yet a nation; rather, an administrative unit. Nepal had begun thinking on national lines only from 1951-52 onwards. It does not have a polity as yet. The primitiveness of the economy these tasks can only be handled if the use of the authority of the throne to achieve these tasks was available.

BP had foreseen, at the time of his return from exile, that 1979 would be a year for democratic possibilities in Nepal. This turned out to be true. After his return from abroad, he found an imminent explosive situation. 'Back to the village' campaign of the Government and activities of Rastravadi Swatantra Vidyarthi Mandal (officially sponsored students' body) had created a situation which were intolerable for the masses. Students of Tribhuvan University had come out on the streets, demanding dissolution of the Government-sponsored students organisation. Although their demand was fulfilled, it did not ease the situation. Anti-government agitations engulfed the whole country in no time. Mobs set fire to the buildings of Government owned newspapers—the *Gorkhapatra* and the *Rising Nepal* in Kathmandu. Unofficial estimates put forty persons having lost their lives in police firing. Leaders like BP, Ganesh Man Singh,

K.P. Bhattarai and Kesar Jung Rai Majhi were promptly put behind the bars.

When it was found that students unrest, instead of getting abated, was taking a violent turn, King Birendra constituted a Royal Commission to look into the problem. Justice Iswari Raj Misra as its member was sent to BP for talks. Justice Misra writes in his memoir, "He (BP) seemed to be relieved by my visit. While discussing he said, "students strike is not so important, what it has revealed is of greater significance. There is dissatisfaction for the present Government among the people. His majesty must decide whether he wants bloodshed first then a dialogue, but if the situation gets out of control, there may not be a chance for a dialogue."

Justice Misra adds, "I said once a revolution starts no one can tell what will be its consequences, new leaders might emerge, people like you might be pushed to the background, or even might get killed." Without a flicker BP replied,"I have come to Nepal risking my life because the country is in danger. I am not afraid to die. At this point if I get killed the King and the country will disappear with me." Justice Misra then said, "In order to satisfy politicians and public, do you think a new constituent assembly should be instituted to frame a new constitution?" To this his reply was: "that is not necessary, what is more important is the practical implementation with some modifications in the constitution."

NATIONAL REFERENDUM

In the midst of this confusion, King Birendra announced on 24th May 1979 his plans for national referendum on the question of political system: whether people wanted a reformed partyless Panchayat System or a Multi-Party System. On the question of referendum there were differences of opinion amongst the stalwarts of the Nepali Congress. Ganesh Man Singh and K.P. Bhattarai argued that in the interest of a fair poll, a general amnesty should be given to all the political prisoners. BP all along maintained a reconciliatory approach. He said, "I do not make this a condition precedent to referendum. My colleagues emphasised this more than I do, but they too have not made this a condition." Finally, on 13th April 1980, the King belatedly announced, the grant of amnesty for political prisoners. BP welcomed it calling it as "king's best gift to the people". BP's stand of not entertaining any conditions before referendum was criticised by his friends and foes alike. But at a time like that when political inactivity which had remained dormant for 19 long years, the party members were just gearing their limited resources to fight election. BP thought such conditionalities might provide the monarch with an excuse to postpone whatever little liberal measures he had offered.

BP did not want to contemplate a situation where the King goes back on his commitment about referendum. "When the king announced a referendum it was total vindication of our rights, the line which we had unitedly pursued with perseverance. And when we have achieved our objective, when we have made the King say that, after all, there is an alternative to the system which his father initiated, the King has recognised the primacy of the people in the decision making process I do not want to say anything that will vicissitude the atmosphere." He took this stand because he was quite optimistic about the outcome of the referendum. "An overwhelming majority of the people will vote for multi-party system. And although we are not going for a united front with other parties, we seek their co-operation. Let me tell you something else : Nepali Congress isn't even issuing a party whip. The policy is to let everyone consult his own conscience before casting the ballot."

While explaining the situation in the country, he said, "The most important issue before the nation is the referendum. All other issues are of secondary importance. Therefore it is the patriotic duty of all of us to see that it is held as early as possible and it is held in the atmosphere of peace and tranquillity. You cannot hold an election properly when law and order is not maintained. The Government's responsibility is primarily twofold— to hold the referendum and to maintain law and order. In the context of the referendum which will decide even the fate of the Government itself, the status of this Government is that of a care-taker. It is politically unsound and also unethical for a care taker Government to try to prolong itself by delaying the holding of the referendum on which hinges the stability of the nation through the initiation of the process of democratisation."

BP requested all the nationalists and democratic elements in the body politic to come under a disciplined political organisation which in the then political context was none other than Nepali Congress. "The experience of nineteen years of authoritarian rule, which not only deprived the people of their human and democratic rights but also enfeebled our national character to the extent that Nepal has become vulnerable to foreign machinations endangering its national integrity, has taught us that the party that aspires to rescue the nation from the present predicament and ensure stability and progress must belong to its dedicated members with total loyalty to its ideal of nationalism, democracy and socialism. All those who share this common purpose with us are welcome to join us in this noble cause."

The results of referendum reaffirmed the partyless Panchayat system, with fifty-four per cent of the votes caste in its favour. Kathmandu was agog with the rigging scandal. Though BP knew all this, he said, "I cannot say that it (referendum) has been rigged. I accept the verdict of the people in accordance with democratic norms." BP knew that the task before the country was enormous and the transformation from monarchy to democracy by constitutional means could not be achieved by creating obstacles. That is the reason why he adopted a policy of no compromise and no confrontation. He said, "We shall not compromise on the issue of democracy and we shall not adopt the line of confrontation with the King. This is why I said no confrontation, no surrender of our rights to fight for democracy in our country. But our fight will not be of the nature of a confrontation with the King."

The Royal proclamation of 21st May 1980 announced that a constitutional reform commission would be set up. King said, "We had already proposed changes to be brought about in the Panchayat polity. In addition, we propose to consider the advice we hope to receive from various segments of our society and bring about necessary amendments in our constitution in near future."[4] Within eight days of this proclamation, the King nevertheless, promulgated the Freedom of Speech and Publication Ordinance which forbade, "All publicity work done in the name of any political party or organisation or in any other form, nor can speeches be made and reading material published in the name of such political groupings."[5]

BP was of the opinion that under the situation that prevailed those days, it would be difficult to have a constitution which would motivate the people to bring out the best in them for the task of nation building. He vehemently opposed it right from its inception saying: "it was harmful for the people as well as the monarch".[6] Since, this plea did not cut much ice with the rulers, he decided to go to the people. He wanted to acquaint the common man the stalemate that had come about in the politics of the country. For quite sometime now, he had also felt the need to make Nepali Congress a cadre based party having a base at the grassroot level. To his friends and comrades he announced, "We have been given a tremendous opportunity to educate the people about my strategy, to tell them why a mass struggle is not appropriate. There has to be ideological clarity and I have to create a political party in the districts parallel to Panchayat system. In this pledge for nation building every village must be occupied with the task of organising the people, of clarifying the basic political issues." Once again the long forgotten democratic process of debate had to be introduced. Later it would be up to the people of Nepal to follow their conscience and decide what was good for the country. Why could Nepalese King and politicians not believe that for Nepal to survive both were important. Mutual co-operation was the order of the day. It was for the people to see that in spite of the opinions of all the earlier nominated Prime Ministers like Kirti Nidhi Bist, Matrika Prasad Koirala, Tulsi Giri, Narendra Prasad Rijal, Surya Bahadur Thapa, that partyless Panchayat system was best for Nepal, did not last for long. The propaganda that nationalism and democracy could not be maintained under multi-party system proved within a short period, how phoney it was. As was the idea that Panchayat system was peculiar to the Nepalese people and was not less democratic than the democratic system obtaining in any of the rich countries.

As L.R. Baral writes, "With all blames put on him following the defeat of multi-party side in the referendum, BP's charisma suffered a considerable set-back, but he once again emerged as unquestionable leader of Nepali Congress. Koirala was equally praised for his intellect and maligned for his miscalculations and 'intransigence'. Moreover, he had been criticised as the most contradictory politician who, for all practical purposes, could neither comprehend Nepal's political context nor did he ever try to take his political stand to a logical end."[7] He further writes, "In 1968, he was released from prison presumably with the hope that he would give fair trial to the party's decision to accept the development of the constitution under the guidance of the King. Not satisfied with the 1968 decision of the party, he, however reverted to the line of confrontation, which he advocated and practised from India since 1969. When he found that his pressure tactic was not going to pay any dividends to him he made his national reconciliation offer of 1976." To this criticism one can only add BP was not a Pandit who could foresee the future. He could only analyse a situation as it arose and find a solution to a problem in a democratic way.

In November 1981, the doctors had given their verdict. BP was afflicted not only by his thirty-five year old throat cancer, but also with lung cancer and malignant growth in the glands which he suffered from 1977 onwards.

BP by now knew that slowly he was slipping out of life. He had started saying, "I don't have long to live and I would be happy to see the beginning. Democracy is a process, it evolves. I will be happy if the strategy for economic development is properly formulated and implementation of those policies are initiated. History does not come to an end with the establishment of democracy. It is the beginning and it is everybody's duty to work for this beginning."[8]

BP had returned to the capital after the first phase of his extensive tour for political reawakening in the interior villages of Nepal, when King Birendra announced the date for filing nomination papers for the elections, even before announcing the date on which these were to be held.

Why was this urgency shown by the rulers? It was due to lack of confidence. All over the kingdom it was felt that the King's intention was to push the Nepali Congress to the walls. BP's tour had been attracting large numbers of people. People from all walks of life would flock to see and hear him, the charismatic leader who had after devoting a full life to their service having almost won a reprieve from death itself to serve them. BP the most venerated leader of his time whom the King had charged for "Treason, for selling his country to India and corruption". His popularity showed that common man in Nepal did not believe in the slander pandered by the palace. The young monarch learned of this quite early. But BP's assessment was different. He observed, "Well, perhaps this is wishful thinking on my part to say that the entire constitutional exercise, beginning from the national referendum to general elections, was initiated by the King, if it was a sincere exercise, to induce elements like us, genuine nationalist democrats, who had remained outside the political system to participate in the system. The King gave substantial concessions to the people, universal adult franchise, direct election, the cabinet's answerability to parliament—in fact, most of the basic democratic rights. However, he retained certain emergency powers. All this was done to get our support, not necessarily that of Nepali Congress alone but democratic support in general. When we decided to boycott the May 1981 general elections the King's purpose was not served and he had to call upon the same man Surya Bahadur Thapa, to form the Government", (17th, 19th December, 1981). The general feeling just before the elections was that Prime Minister Thapa was stage-managing the show. The stipulation that a candidate must enroll himself as a member of one of the six Panchayat controlled class organisations and be under pledge to subscribe to the principles of partyless Panchayat. How BP, who in the beginning itself had declared no preconditions before the elections, could subscribe to such conditions laid down by the palace? He says, "We are forced" at the same time he cautioned his comrades and people of Nepal, "Extremism of either right or left is a hurdle to the democratic development of the country."

During this crucial phase in the struggle, BP the crusader for democracy and freedom was well aware of the dangers involved and was keen that every peaceful avenue should be explored to bring about democratic transformation of the Nepalese society. He was asked, "Don't you think your non-participation in the general elections will close all your options except that of politics of conflict? Where do you go from here, now that you have decided to stay away from the election? BP replies, "I think if I had joined the system, Thapa's options are limited. M.P. Koirala's (former nominated PM) options are limited but not my options because I am with the people." The strategy evolved during the struggle was unique in itself in the sense that it was neither an active Satyagraha nor a passive one. The Nepali Congress did not take to active Satyagraha, as it would have meant booth capturing or not letting the voters to go to the polling stations. Since people in general were encouraged to participate in the election and make their own choice. Nor was it a passive one. As BP said, "The election, would be meaningful only when the people who had remained outside the prevalent system participate in the election. If the same set of people who have been with the system, in the Panchayat process for the last twenty years, were to be involved in the election then the election is meaningless."[9]

For BP there was no question of participating in the elections if his rights were snatched away from him. If he did not have a right to put across his point of view through expression and through organisation, then his contesting an election or getting elected had no meaning.

He further said, "This constitution is not bold enough to take note of the rising expectations of the people. We are the representatives of the people so we thought we should be betraying the trust they had reposed in us if we accepted the constitution and fought the elections. That is why we are not participating." Some leaders and party workers of the Nepali Congress wanted to fight the elections and were hopeful of winning it. Many held this view in spite of the common knowledge about the rigging of the Referendum. BP knew that this trend was not good for the country if it had to follow the true democratic traditions. He doubted the holding of fair elections. He had taken the earlier Referendum results lying low, mainly for the sake of wider interests of the country. He thought sooner or later people would themselves see to it that rigging was not done. Till then he had to go to the people and explain to them the value of the democratic traditions.

REFERENCES

1. *Udghatan Bhasan,* Prime Minister B.P. Koirala at the first conference of Nepal Tarun Dal. Kathmandu. 15 Dec. 1961 Gorkhaptra Press.
2. Tarun Prakashan, 1979, 4-6 (2036).
3. M.J. Akbar, *Sunday,* Calcutta, 24, 1979.
4. *The Hindustan Times,* 14 April, 1980.
5. *Ibid.,* 15 May, 1980.
6. *Ibid.,* 31 May, 1980.
7. L.R. Basal, *Nepali Politics of Referendum : A Study of Groups Personalities and Trends,* pp. 173-74, Vikas, New Delhi.
8. *Rising Nepal,* 10 April, 1980, Kathmandu.
9. The decision of not participating in the elections showed BP was again following the footsteps of Mahatma. By 1919 Gandhi with his non-violent, non-co-operation weapons which were psychological and ethical one. Later, Salt Satyagraha campaign was a symbolic resistance in order to stir energies of the nation. As we know it rekindled the light of patriotism in the hearts of the Indian people.

8

BP'S ROMANTICISM

Every time the name of B.P. Koirala is mentioned one gets the impression that he was a politician through and through. But his writings, ideas, vision and the impression of those who rallied around him reveal a different story. He was a social thinker, a philosopher, a dreamer, a crusader and a writer. He cherished ideas and tried to transform them into reality. However one may say he was a disorganised man. Let us look at him as a family man.

FAMILY MAN

Their marriage was an interesting event. In the year 1937, Sushila was a student of class IX in Theosophical School, in Kamakshya, Varanasi. After hearing from her father, BP went to have a 'look' at the girl, and the next thing which he promptly did was to send a cable to her father fixing the date of marriage. Horrified father sent messages requesting postponement of the date. BP was adamant. He insisted on the 4th February for marriage to be ceremonised or no marriage at all. Mischievously he recalls it was solemnised on that day. Only a small group, two of his brothers and a sister, could join the ceremony. After their marriage, Sushila says, "We would be moving from one house to another, I don't even remember how many houses we shifted to and from—Kedar Ghat, Nirala Niwas, Hasana, Dhoodvinayak, and a few more places."

About Sushila he wrote: "My wife is much interested in dance and she used to take me to performance. I will not say that she herself is a great dancer. When she is on stage her expressions are so spontaneous and natural that they make up for whatever deficiency she may have in art or technique. Thanks to her, I have seen all the celebrated ballets—Russian, English. I have also seen all the renowned Indian dancers perform. My preferences are of course for Bharat Natyam, Kathakali and Odissi. Paying a tribute to his family and others for their affection, he said, "The tremendous love, affection, respect that I have received from my people, my friends and family members is a gift worthy of the gods." Small gestures and little concerns would make this simple man boundlessly happy. Once a group of villagers from Terai had come to see him. When it was getting late for them, he reminded them that they had a long way to treck back. But they insisted for his photograph which they would take to their people otherwise they "would abuse us for not meeting BP". He was overwhelmed by such gestures.

Paying rich tribute to his life-partner, Shushila who enriched his life in many ways, BP says, "She appears to me even today as fresh as on the day I married her, partly because I have lived away from her most of our married life. I was in prison or on tour or in exile, I did not have enough of her companionship, so she retains the same attraction for me, she has been a great asset to me. There is a spiritual quality in her that sustains me."

Both husband and wife had similar temperamental affinity. She too was basically a withdrawing type. Happy within her limited circle of intimate friends. BP would deliberately avoid big receptions and limelight. When asked by Bhola Chatterji how does it make you feel to be known as a man with charisma for last thirty years, BP in his humble way replies, "No, I think I have received more love and affection, personal things than respect as a leader. You see, people call me San daju, which means little elder brother, so I lead a family group, a very big family no doubt. But I have received brickbats also by virtue of my position in the party. If I had been pampered all along, perhaps, I might have lost my head."

SUSHILA AGAINST HIS BECOMING PRIME MINISTER

It seems Sushila was dead set against her husband becoming Prime Minister of Nepal. On many occasions in those days she did not participate in some of the programmes organised to felicitate the first democratically elected Prime Minister. Later, however, she acceded to her husband's wishes. A letter from Sushila Koirala to Jai Prakash Narayan explains her attitude so well. "You have written that he wants to become the Prime Minister of Nepal. Instead of accusing him like that you should have allowed him to die in his last illness."[1] BP later admitted, "She had to suffer more than I have. She had become completely grey-haired". This was because she did not know for about two years whether her husband was alive or dead in the prison. In the meanwhile she had to brave many social and financial difficulties. During those days, being wife of BP had its own adversities. After meeting his prematurely grey-haired wife behind the prison walls, BP took to introspection—what right has he to bring so much of suffering to his near and dear ones, just because he was committed to an ideology? For BP, such ethical doubts were momentary. He would willy-nilly get into his political activities.

It could not be otherwise for he was born to be a politician. As he had said, "Politics was in our blood". The mere thought that he was born in the family of Krishna Prasad who had died in Rana prison gave him the will and energy to fight. He himself said, "I couldn't have been other than what I am. My life is a series of reactions to these facts of existence. In wordly terms, in the eyes of the people, I have undergone great hardship in life a life of deprivation, hunger, imprisonment, sometimes in inhuman conditions, serious illnesses. I have no sense of suffering. Any other kind of life would have been not only boring but coarse also."

ROMANTICISM

BP elaborates on his romanticism and says, "You cannot bear the agony of life without a touch of romanticism to sustain you, that is what I feel. I am bit of a dreamer, too. In prison I was kept for six months in total isolation. My hands and legs were loosely fetterred and I saw no man, only heard distant voices. I used to dream about how to escape this or that. After a few hours, I used to realise that I was dreaming, not merely due to personal strains. I think you need a certain amount of romanticism in your psychology to bear the strain of all the suffering around you, the suffering of women and the emaciated children."

The same blend of romanticism is reflected when he says "as a socialist I am searching for better laws to bind the people, as a writer I am breaking all the laws. My friends find it difficult to reconcile these two. They say my writings do not mirror my political struggles. That is because I am not a politician when I write."

Being an attractive man with romantic disposition and a charming personality he attracted members of the opposite sex wherever he went. When cornered by his friend Bhola Chatterji, he says, "My experience is that there would be very few people who did not have affairs other than the relations with their wives. I am a normal being; from that point of view I had affairs. But the permanent, abiding moorings of life are there in her" (Sushila).

A man who spent more than four years in prison in India, about eleven years in Nepal and seven years in exile, had got ample time and opportunity to reflect about his own life. He says, "I would have produced more writings expressing my ideas, my philosophy of politics cogently or I could have contributed more to building up the democratic forces in Nepal. There is a constant feeling that I may not live long, and I have to do a lot before I die, but the death has no terror for me."

BELIEVER OF KARMA PHILOSOPHY

Early in life he had come to realise that in a poor country one fought not for power but for establishing basic values and norms, and for these one has to have spiritual content in the struggle. Otherwise it becomes simply impossible for both the leader as well as the struggle to survive. This approach also gave him the conviction to say, "So far as I am concerned, in personal terms it is not success or failure that matters. If in your heart of hearts you feel that you have done your best, you have staked all that you are capable of, this gives you satisfaction and that is what I feel. I have not succeeded in the generally understood sense of the term. But when I see people achieving success rather cheap, I don't think they get any spiritual satisfaction. You are spiritually more satisfied when you find yourself making efforts even if you fail. I think this is what has happened to me". He made his views further clear, in 1952 in a letter to Bhola Chatterji where he wrote about Jai Prakash Narayan, "His incentive to goodness is full of flaws and I do not understand the need of discarding materialism in favour of spiritualism in order to achieve good existence... I never suffer from frustration. I, on the other hand, suffer from over-abundance of frivolity. I believe in taking things easy, almost in Jocose mood... There is no frustration for me."

Many riddles get solved when one looks back as to why BP risked going to the gallows than remaining a free man on Indian soil. He and his comrades knew that if they remained in India they would be unhappy. Now it was time to go back to their country. Once the decision was taken there was no going back. A man of iron will as he was, he went ahead. No amount of persuasion from friends and well-wishers made any difference.

A COMPULSIVE LOVER OF HUMAN FREEDOM

BP loved human freedom so much that he went to plead even a case for euthanasia: "Man has a right to commit suicide, particularly when he is suffering from an incurable disease and he is a burden to his family and also to himself. I support suicide but not when one commits it out of sheer frustration. I am an advocate of euthanasia. In fact I have told my people that if I get a paralytic stroke or if I am down with terminal cancer, I should be administered some injection to put me to eternal rest."[2] Who could be a better person to plead the case for euthanasia than BP who lived life under the shadow of cancer.

It is this love for freedom which even the four walls of jail could not subdue. When no other option was open, writing became a passion for him—Narendra, Munariya, Gauri, Pulome, Suminma, Somdutt, David, Narayan, Rekha speak volumes. BP wrote his novels as he lived the life of his characters and left for posterity some sensitive psychological novels. A creative writer looks to the world with his own eyes, feelings, aspirations and jest for life. This again depends upon his experiences. BP's novels and short stories dramatise and explain tensions and duality in the inner life of an individual. Like Sartre, to some extent, he remains committed to individual freedom. BP was trying to unmask hypocrisy and injustices. The methodological and moral legacy of Sartre's existentialism which BP has in a small way tried to fulfill.

Like his love for freedom, nature gets reflected in most of his creative works. His love for nature is clearly reflected. When he writes, "If you are not overwhelmed by the sight of the rise of sun over Tiger Hills, if you cannot sleep well after watching the sunset from Chaupatty, you have missed something fundamental. If you are not moved by serene grandeur of the sea at Puri, then you have missed something in life. God resides in poetry, God resides in dreaming. You can't explain him through science, through materialism, God is a spiritual experience." Once this was achieved, a person would become sensitive to other people's needs and feelings."

BP was accused of being an atheist by some. They even went to the extent of saying that he would convert the temple of Pashupatinath into a museum. All his life, he faced groups who would come up with vague charges against him. But he remained undaunted by his critics and admirers alike.

In his opinion, "First of all nobody has defined for men what he means by God. But that part of existence in which man starts composing poems, when he is filled with oceanic feeling, when he sees the vastness of the universe, when he sees its beauty, the flowers, that is the experience of God and divinity." Although initially a Marxist, he did not embrace Marx's dialectical materialism: "I do not say, there is absolutely no truth in that. Man is a multi-dimensional entity. The mistake Marx made was that he treated man as an economic being, who is interested only in his economic life. I will not say that there is no truth in that, but it is very inadequate portraiture. Man is an economic being but he is something more. What is that something more? You might say man is God's creation. I think yes, but still more, the dimensions are many. Secondly, man is never motivated by the considerations of bread only. The stomach is not the sole instigator of his activities."

REFERENCES

1. Jai Prakash Narayan papers, Nehru Museum Library, New Delhi.
2. *Towards A New Society: Congress for Cultural Freedom*, Jai Prakash Narayan, p. 25.

9

COMMUNISTS AND BP

Before we look into BP's relationship with the Communists of Nepal, let us first have a glance at the origin and politics of the Communist Party of Nepal. The birth of Nepal Communist Party is credited to five young dedicated revolutionaries who had founded it on the 15th September, 1949. They were Niranjan Govind, Narayan Vilash, Nara Bahadur, Durga Devi and Pushpalal. Initially some like-minded youths, inspired by the great revolutionary changes all through the south and south-east Asia, had started some agitational activities in different parts of Nepal. It is said that Biratnagar mill *majdoor* strike of 1947 was originally planned by some of them, specially by Man Mohan Adhikari, before finally its leadership passed over to the Rastriya Congress.

FOOTHOLDS OF COMMUNIST PARTY

The overthrow of the Rana followed by unsettled conditions of the country gave fresh opportunities to the Communists to build a National Democratic Front with the support of other parties and organizations like the Praja Parishad, Kisan Sangh, Nepal Trade Union, Youth and Women's Federations. The Front became popular amongst the nationalists because of its opposition to the Rana-Congress compromise made in Delhi. The progressive and more radical sections of anti-Rana movement supported it because of the alleged reactionary role played by the Nepali Congress leadership after entering the government. According to Pushpalal, "After the end of Rana regime everybody, including the feudals wanted to join our party. This was so because, the revolutionary section of the people could not digest Delhi Compromise made by the Congress, so they wanted to join us because we consistently fought Delhi Compromise."

Besides, they capitalised on the dissensions on the Delhi Agreement. At its first Congress, the Nepal Communist Party stated, "The ignoble Delhi Compromise of February 1951 has been a failure and non-stable due to a single reason that they could not fulfill any aspirations of the people to the slightest degree."[1]

In addition, the growing economic distress and the acute land problem among the vast body of cultivating labourers in Tarai and eastern hills also provided a wide basis for the front. In spite of physical handicap, ideological inexperience and immaturity of the leadership, the Communist Party was able to gain a strong foothold amongst the poor peasantry and intellectual middle class in towns. This closer contact with the people along with adoption of revolutionary programme enabled the party to outgrow the narrow framework of Nepali politics which consisted of personal wrangles among the leaders and intermittent wire pullings with the palace to get a place in the ministry.

Pushpalal, a member of the Politbureau of the Communist Party of Nepal, said in an interview in 1959, "To an extent Indian government wants to see that the pro-Indian sections besides Nepali Congress gain upper hand. For instance, M.P. Koirala is an out and out pro-Indian. Though BP too is a creation of India he has courage to take an independent stand. Further, under the present conditions, we are supporting the Congress as a liberal force; for instance we support its policy of Birta Abolition. But we are also clear that the present Government cannot work for the National interest f Nepal." Communist Party was interested in establishing peoples republics in Nepal. They accepted the King under duress. When it was said that the ban on Nepal Communist Party would be lifted only if they accepted the King as the head of the state, the Communists reluctantly accepted it. Nepali Congress was thought to be bourgeoisie reactionary party. Much later however it was granted by the Communists that, in the changing world, even the social democrats have certain role to play. This started a series of debates on the validity of democratic socialism. Nepal Communist Party, as we shall see later, suffered from a dichotomy in its relations with Nepali Congress and its leaders. Beni Bahadur Karki much intrigued about the situation prevailing then says, "You must know some things about the palace intrigues of that time. Only those who were pro-Indian or pro-King were asked to form the government. For the King [Tribhuvan] most important consideration was finance. In 1952 he wanted to go to Europe for medical treatment and the person willing to bear all his expenses was most likely to get the Prime Ministership. M.P. Koirala always promised to do so, and he was Tribhuvan's favourite. On the basis of these considerations ministries were formed; every individual began to make a party just to be made a minister sometimes in the royal lottery."

The Communists knew that under the scheme of things prevailing at that time, they could never aspire to form a government. So they devoted their time and energy in building up a mass base. The efforts put up by the leadership and the cadres over the years is now paying rich dividends. Madan Bhandari, General Secretary of the United Nepal Communist Party, today proudly proclaims, "What has happened in Russia and Eastern Europe was an aberration that the scientific socialism has finally come to rest in the safekeeping of the Communist parties of Nepal and India."

Following the uprising of Raksha Dal in January 1952 led by Dr. K.I. Singh, the Congress ministry of M.P. Koirala which was formed in August 1951 declared the Communist Party of Nepal as illegal. This forced the Communists to go underground and carry on their activities under the cover of such mass organisations like the Youth and Kisan Sangh and Peace Councils.

Almost after four years, Prajaparishad, Government of Tanka Prasad Acharya lifted the ban on the Communist Party. In the meanwhile the Communist Party had done a fine work of underground movement in Nepal. When the elections of 1959 came, the party set up 47 candidates, and won four seats to the Pratinidhi Sabha. They polled over 7 per cent of the total votes cast in the election. The Nepal Communist Party from its inception was concentrating on the peasantry, students and youth because it was only through them that they could penetrate the heart of the masses.

It is also widely known that the youth of Nepal are taking a major role of opposition to the regime. Both Nepali Congress and the Communist Party have great hold on the student community. Associations like Nepal Vidyarthi Sangh, Akhil Nepal Swatantra Vidyarthi Union, Rastriya Swatantra Vidyarthi Mandal, are all trying to enlarge their sphere of influence amongst the youth in Nepal.

COMMUNIST MANIFESTO

The communist election manifesto asserted that "during eight years of interim rule there have been continuous infringement of democratic rights of the people. The medieval backwardness of the Nepali peasantry remained unchanged, and economic distress of the villages, unemployment among the urban middle class and administrative nepotism and corruption went from bad to worse." The party programme visualised a peaceful foreign policy with the annulment of unequal treaties and agreements with India and other foreign states and prevention of American infiltration into Nepal. It demanded radical land reforms, rapid development of key and basic industries under the state sector, abolition of feudal land ownership like Rajauta, Birta and Zamindari. It promised encouragement to the growth and development of linguistic minorities, guarantees of religious freedom and providing all sorts of facilities to the pilgrims to their places of pilgrimage. The programme envisaged an unicameral parliament with the power to amend the constitution; organisation of an independent judiciary and public service commission and also the right of the electorate to recall their representative from the parliament.

When asked what factors were playing the most important role in Nepali politics, Tulsilal Amatya has this to say: "Situation creates politics. As you find, the failures of Nepali Congress has given incentive to the communists to grow. It is true that the King too wants to control politics, and it is also true that if the Nepali Congress fails as a result of its policies, power may go then to the King once more. Much depends on how the

Communist Party succeeds in making the people conscious of the political problems and how far it can lead the masses in an organised manner."

As far as their shortsighted nationalism is concerned, Communists unwittingly played the palace game. It is a sad story to recall that the palace and the Communists together in their anti-India tirade thought less of the country and their democratically elected government, and worked more in covert alliance, looking for every opportunity to discredit the Nepali Congress. It was due to this unholy alliance that Ajoya Ghosh, General Secretary of the Communist Party of India, once jokingly told comrade Keshar Jung Rai Majhi "Don't tell me you are planning a Royal Communist Party."

During those decisive days of his Prime Ministership, BP had to do tight-rope walking. The Communists would denounce every step taken by him. As for the Communists he says, "True test of tolerance is to put up with that which you dislike most." BP tolerated the Communists in every possible way. It was only when the dictatorial government started picking up individual Communists and putting them in jail because by this time the Communists had started embarrassing the King by challenging his authority, the Communist Party members realised their vulnerable position. Some top leaders sought refuge in India. Instead of being a ginger group, the Communists could have played a vital role in the development of Nepal if they had formulated a long-term strategy with constructive approach, together with the Nepali Congress. There is no doubt that at least they could have helped preserve the infant democracy in Nepal. After the installation of the Koirala government, the Communist Party directed all its energies in building up anti-India hysteria with the sole desire of discrediting Prime Minister B.P. Koirala government.

In the meanwhile, Chinese activities in Tibet and their claims on certain parts of Nepal's northern border were reported to have caused some differences among the Communist leadership[2] but nothing was available to confirm this report. When pointedly asked, "Do you think that present Chinese invasion in the north has affected your party?" Pushpalal replies, "Not a bit. Our party is getting stronger day by day. Only recently the reactionary parties organised an Everest demand day demonstration. It was only 2000 to 3000 strong and most of the demonstrators were school children. Two days later we organised anti-Gandak demonstration and nearly 50,000 people participated. It was the biggest demonstration ever seen in the valley. We are mustering our strength on Dalda and Gandak issue to organise the people against Indian intervention."[3]

In May 1959, Nepali Congress had unequivocally criticised Chinese imperialist policy of enslavement of Tibet. In March 1960, Prime Minister B.P. Koirala visited China and negotiated an agreement with the Chinese leaders on Nepal's boundary with China. Under this agreement, later a joint team was sent and the boundary demarcated. It was due to the efforts of BP, Marshall Chenyi, Vice Premier and Foreign Minister of China announced his support to "Nepalese people in the event of overt aggression by any foreign power."[4] This change in China's attitude was due to the statesmanship of BP. Later, however, after the dismissal of his ministry, King Mahendra concluded a treaty of friendship with China.

CONGRESS AND COMMUNISTS ON DIVERGENT COURSE

After the takeover by King Mahendra, it was hoped that the Congress and Communist parties would come together and rally against the King, but this did not happen. BP tried his utmost to bring Communists under one platform:

> On several occasions we discussed with the communists in order to thrash out our differences and evolve a common approach to various problems confronting Nepal. We found unbridgeable gulf that separates us is their doctrine of economics. I told them that Nepal's problem was essentially political and that the economic issues were merely dependent on it. They, however, insisted that economic issues were primary and political ones secondary. I put forward a proposal for their consideration. I suggested that they should draw up an economic programme and economic objectives and I was ready to put my signature, declaring my adherence

to it. They in turn should permit me to prepare a political programme and its goal, and both parties—the Nepali Congress and the communists—should adhere to them. I argued since I considered economic issues to be of little consequence in the present Nepalese context, I would without hesitation put my signature jointly with them on their document setting forth the economic programme or economic goals, or a plan for new economic relationships.

I stand for land reforms. After all, who will not? Even the King is, I am for social justice. I am also for the end of economic exploitation. There are two tests for my economic plan; one whether it promotes social justice. Whether we call it an economic revolution or transformation, but they constitute the real test for success of an economic plan. Economic revolution is not a sudden affair, it is a long process. The communists readily agreed to my proposal and asked me to formulate concretely my political objectives.

I explained that democracy meant the sovereignty of the people. It should both in theory and practice be vested in the people. If this is accepted, the people must have right to elect their own government. The people, therefore, should have a real choice, to elect among various political parties and individuals. They must have the freedom of organization, freedom of speech and civil liberties. This will naturally lead to a multi-party system in the country. The communists agreed to all the above essential ingredients of democracy, except the one, namely, a multi-party system. If this is accepted as an essential ingredient of democracy it would entail by implication the denial of the communist system already established in various countries. My proposal was not accepted by them. This reveals clearly that the vital issue today in Nepal is strictly political."[5]

Reflecting on the controversies and misunderstandings, BP was to say:

Do you or don't you accept people as the most important factor for change? Do you or don't you accept that they have to move first. If the reply is in the affirmative, you have to accept the demand for people's politics. After all, what is politics? It is the management of man. A dictatorship manages them as cattles. Democracy is the management of the people through an institution representing their own will. The people are negative factors in dictatorial kind of politics, but in democracy they are all positive ones. In the one people do not develop a sense of responsibility towards the national task; in the other they cannot escape it. Economics is management of things. In democracy this vests with the people."

Further he said:

King Birendra shared with the communists a common belief that economics occupies the centre of Nepal's problems. I do not mean by this statement that he is a communist and believes in the doctrine of the economic interpretation of history. I only mean to say that the King in the interest of his own authoritarian rule has come to share this doctrine espoused by the communists, who on their part derive their ideas from outside and not from the Nepalese reality or their own experience.

BP had all along emphasized, "we want constitutional monarchy, but there have been different phases of monarchy. At one time, there were two monarchs—one was living in Delhi, another was sitting on the throne. And for one hundred and four years the monarch was virtually a prisoner, an exalted prisoner. I was a prisoner in the ordinary prison and he was a prisoner in the palace. It is not enough to ask whether I want monarchy or not. You must be definite about what type of monarch you want."[6]

Communists too maintained that change in Nepal should come in a constitutional way "but in case obstacles arise, they shall not hesitate to take other means than constitutional. If force is used, force will be applied." When asked about the role of the King in Nepali politics, Manmohan Adhikari replied, "His role is not sharply evident of course, the present constitution is very limited and gives too many discretionary powers to the king. We accepted this constitution because we were not strong enough to oppose the Royal award in 1958. But the constitution must be changed through organised movement of the people."[7]

About Nepal Communist Party's attitude towards Nepali Congress BP had said, "The pro-Moscow groups have been sometimes very friendly and sometimes very hostile. It is more or less the same with pro-Peking groups. The whole problem with pro-Peking groups, I don't know whether they are pro-Peking or not, but they call themselves Maoist, is that there are five or six groups. They fight among themselves more bitterly then against others. And there are severe differences between the pro-Peking and pro-Moscow lines. So far as Nepal's politics is concerned they are not much of consequence at present. They may have the potentiality but that is about all. In the context of the referendum or of the election that would follow they are of no consequence.

The Naxalites are opposed to referendum, but in this they are one with those who are not interested in the democratic process because they feel they cannot come to power that way. I don't think the Naxalites have any strategy to power. Their goal is to create chaos."[8]

The left in Nepal, whether the 'old' or the 'new' brand, would have provided leadership only if they had been less confused, in their petty solace they forgot their higher goals.

On foreign policy issue, the Nepal Communist Party's position was: "We believe in the policy of nationalism and neutrality i.e., non-alignment with either power blocks. We however, strongly felt that Indian Government interferes too much in Nepal's foreign and internal affairs, and does not keep in mind the fact of Nepal's sovereign independent status. There are many instances of Indian expansionism. Our problem is we have to oppose India even though we have best intentions to carry on friendly relations with her." The Nepal Communist Party has been consistent in their anti-India stand. In their exuberance to catch up with short publicity gains they have shown immaturity. It goes to the credit of the leaders of the Nepali Congress that while in power they restrained themselves, from using foreign policy issues lightly. Leo Rose has rightly written: "B.P. Koirala government has been virtually unique in the annals of modern Nepali politics during its first year in office, because of its restraint in using foreign policy issues to bolster its domestic position."[9]

It was only during the elections that M.M. Adhikari saw the writings on the wall and decided to support BP for restoration of multi-party system. He proposed that a multi-party restoration committee be formed under the Chairmanship of BP.

Dr. Baral writes, "The post-referendum declaration period demonstrated that M.M. became a popular name along with BP though the former's organizational base and charisma was no match for the latter's. The other leftist factions looked at M.M. with disclaim because of the rapproachement established by him with NC." Right from the beginning the fate of all united front governments in Nepal were of short tenure. It started with Nepali Congress—Rana coalition government, followed by Tanka Prasad Acharya's ministry and in 1957 Dr. K.I. Singh's multi-party Government. During those chaotic period, the Nepali Congress was the only party which could have brought together all divergent groups under one banner, as it had an ideological binding, 'socialism'. Unfortunately each group played a game with a shortsighted approach and a revolution was lost.

BP's PRAGMATIC APPROACH

To the ruling group's charge that he was hand-in-glove with India and that his loyalty to Nepal is doubtful, BP stated, "I must be clearly understood that I am for Nepal. But at the same time we shall have to maintain a friendly, most cordial and intimate relations with India. We just cannot whisk away the fact of geography. With all respects to the patriotic sentiments of a Nepali, we cannot afford to be anti-India. We cannot take up the cause of those countries which are anti-India. I am not a stooge of anybody. I am not pro-India, pro-China or pro-America, I am pro-Nepal."

BP was critical of India on several counts. "The mistake of India has been that of a poor country wanting to adopt the model of Russia and America. It should have adopted the model given by Mahatma Gandhi, small-scale, agro-industry catering to the needs of village folks. This is what we want in our country. Industry that takes care of the tools of production, like improving primitive designs of the plough, improving the breed of the cattle, the need of the people to clothe themselves, improving their energy resources, like the conservation of cowdung for energy purposes."

BP whole-heartedly believed that 'small is beautiful'. Yet he did little to bring about much needed economic transformation in Nepali society. He could have started some movement like Mahatma Gandhi's Charkha. A man of BP's stature could have given a simple call and people would have followed him. He did not do it basically because he was a disorganised man. When the time was ripe he missed the opportunity. One could also say that though BP had this model for economic upliftment of his country close to his heart, he could not get sufficient time to implement it. About the model, BP says, "the first to conceive of a different model was Gandhi in India, and Jai Prakash Narayan today; and now there are thinkers coming up in England, people like the author of a beautiful book, *Small is Beautiful*, E.F. Schumacher. He coined the phrase, *intermediate technology* for the third world, technology that does not need great infusions of capital. This is the model we will adopt, and not the American model, which we cannot afford in our country."

According to BP democracy and economic development are not contradictory concepts. They are complementary concepts. As a matter of fact he believed that economic development starts from politics. In a written answer to a fortnightly *National Star*, BP airs his feelings: "In the total absence of democratic rights, in the condition of denial to the people of the constitutional and inherent right of free expression, all those who try to raise their voice of protest against such a insufferable state of affairs at a grave risk to themselves and their families are the representative of the people and as such represent the democratic cause. For the last nineteen years I have an honour to belong to a handful of such brave men, young and not so young, students and non-students who have given me their love, affection and confidence. I speak for them, some of whose cries were stiffled with gunmen's bullets or strangled under their boots. I consider myself to belong to that company of courageous people—my party men or otherwise—who did not knuckle under or did not go down on their knees before the display of illegal force which is tyranny. All of them represent democracy. I am one of them."

Democracy alone cannot deliver goods to the people. Development is equally necessary. Hence, according to the Nepali Congress: "We need democracy for development purpose also... We export human beings rather than goods. So the human materials is not being used in our development. In our country we want to have small industries where we can employ many people, rather than employ a small number of people and big machines." Not only that according to BP, "Both democracy and its corollary institutions will be safer with a constitutional monarch, as elected person will always have the propensity to think of himself as a real representative of the people." The worst of the world's big dictators were elected people. Hitler was elected, Mussolini was elected and so were others. I do not believe there is an incompatibility between democracy, socialism and constitutional monarchy." His justification for monarchy was that, "During the transition period, the king will have a role to play. I always give the example of Spain. If the monarchy had not been restored in Spain I don't think the transition from Franco's fascism to democracy would have been possible so smoothly."

Being asked by Thedore Jacquency "You said you believe that democracy is indispensable for development, would you elaborate on this?" BP simply replied. "It is like this: what are the resources for our development purposes? We would accept outside aid, but that can only have marginal impact on our development efforts we have to channelise our own resources."[10]

BP had full faith in his party men. "It is not that party men are not with me. I have given them a new approach and they are fully satisfied with it. As for criticism about me I am quite used to it. My conscience is clear, my aim is clear. Those who criticise me today will realise later how wrong they were."[11]

Of and on, death had awaited at his doorsteps but "my ideals, my faith in democracy and love for my people kept me alive." BP had told the King, before going for his treatment abroad, "I have to keep faith of my people. There are large numbers of political prisoners who are facing similar charges so I think my place is with them. I am once again placing myself at the disposal of the King." He was one person in Nepal who had many opportunities to compromise on his principles in exchange for a position of power and a comfortable life. But to those ideals and principles which he had embraced early in life he remained steadfast.

Another ideal close to BP's heart was that of human rights. Man must have his fundamental human rights to live a decent life. Any planning that bypasses the man, according to him was no planning at all. A man who with the rising sun walks out to his field with plough on his shoulders to work the whole day long was the true citizen of a poor country. He was proud of Nepali cultivator who with his limited inputs produced more rice per acre than many countries with more advanced devices. Our development starts when we mobilise people. We have manpower and land. We have to mobilise this manpower, he would say.

BP pointed out during his Prime Ministership the difficulties and strains of transition to development and progress. Politically, "while it is natural that localism might gain some added vitality insofar as elections are fought on the basis of locality and the Government is formed on the results of the election, we have by conscious effort, if necessary, to keep ourselves free from this narrow feeling as far as we can." Furthermore, "There are certain similar anti-national elements also which by means of extreme slogans and destructive activities in the midst of our uncertainties arising out of our present transition period make more complicated our problems of development... The Nepali Congress must try to bind all other national forces into a single strand by means of which the problems of present day revolution may be solved, and the country may proceed on its appointed path of economic development and national reconstruction... while it is true that there are unfortunately people in the country who are inclined to belittle the significance of the constructive activities now proceeding. I feel that the chief reason for such obscurantism is narrowness of mind and, in one word, parochialism. I need not say that I whole-heartedly believe that we have entirely to eschew parochialism, provincialism or localism for some years, and have to adopt a national view point throughout the period that we are laying the foundation of the economic development in the country... our basic problem is to develop economic base for the country. In a planned economy we cannot give any consideration for local regional factors. We cannot be influenced to change our economic plan on those considerations specially when we have very limited resources. In a planned economy, centrifugal tendency becomes predominant and that again constitutes a problem not only to us, but to the whole world. Anyway our first responsibility today is to build up the basic economic structure and even parliament is not conscious of the hugeness of our task."[12]

He further says, "The very fact that now there is an opposition in parliament proves that democratic ways have begun. I must confess that though opposition inside parliament behaves quite well, opposition outside tends to be irresponsible. In spite of it our experience of the last one year, makes me hopeful to say that the new institution has been well adopted". Deputy Chairman of Mahasabha, Kamal Rana, commenting on the situation prevailing at that time says, "I find more stability. There is now a homogeneous cabinet. The government I think is moving very fast with reforms so that people are lagging behind. The success of this government depends how far these legislations would be successful in their purpose."

BP says, "Nepal herself is at the crossroad. One road leads to progress—to development—and to a bright future. The other is the path of downfall—a road leading to dark abyss of a futureless chaos. Everybody is asking himself the question along which of these two roads is the Nepali Congress leading the country. Are we not able to learn the lessons that history teaches? I certainly believe that we do understand the implications of history, and our plans are to lead the country along the road to our brightest future. That is why we have gathered here today from the remotest corners of the country with high aspirations, to discuss all matters which concern the welfare of Nepal and her people."[13]

It is also true that Nepali Congress from its inception has been a movement. For the past thirty years it never took the character of a party. There is no doubt it was guided by certain principles and philosophy. Later however, the overthrow of the Panchayat system became its objective. It was never believed that Panchayat system would collapse like a house of cards.

REFERENCES

1. *Jan Andolan Ma Nepal Kamyunist Party.*
2. Pushpalal and Tulsilal Amatya members of Politbureau. Pushpalal was regarded as the most dynamic political figure ranking in popularity next only to Ganesh Man Singh. He too was known as Mahila Daju (second brother) affectionately by his comrades and friends. A humane and soft-spoken person—a dedicated man. After the coup he led life of an emigre, in Calcutta, Varanasi and Gorakhpur, co-ordinating and organising Nepali students.
3. An interview with Anirudha Gupta, 1960, unpublished monograph.
4. New China News Agency Report, 6 October, 1962
5. Interview given to *Young India Weekly*, by B.P. Koirala, Delhi, June, 1973.
6. Bhola Chatterji interviews B.P. Koirala just before he went back to Nepal, *Sunday*, Calcutta, Dec. 4, 1977.
7. Anirudha Gupta, "Nepali Politics : A Decade of Doldrum" (unpublished monograph).
8. Sunday Magazine, Amrita Bazar Patrika, Calcutta, July 29, 1979.
9. Leo Rose, *Nepali Strategy for Survival*, Oxford Press, 1971, p. 229.
10. *National Star*, July, 1979.
11. B.P. talks to Theodore Jacuqency just before returning to Nepal.
12. Interview given to Anirudha Gupta (unpublished monograph).
13. Presidential Address by Shri B.P. Koirala, delivered at the seventh Annual Session of the Nepali Congress at Kathmandu on May 7, 1960.

10

JAWAHARLAL, INDIAN SOCIALISTS AND BP

Contrary to his wishes Pandit Jawaharlal Nehru had seen Congress Socialist Party break away from the Congress. In the meanwhile Pandit Nehru's views towards the left were getting manifested in different ways. He wrote, "Leftism in India was an infantile phenomenon, a collection of odd elements united by frustration and dislike of the Congress."[1] He expressed similar sentiments regarding Socialists as well. In his letter to Sardar Vallabh Bhai Patel he wrote, "As for the Socialists, they continue to show an amazing lack of responsibility and reconstructive bend of mind. They seem to be all frustrated and going mentally to pieces."[2]

The decision of the Congress Socialist Party to leave the Congress was a staggering blow to the prestige of Jawaharlal Nehru. Parting of ways with Jai Prakash Narayan was not a simple affair. Expressing his concern he wrote to Patel... "apt to go astray, very often acts in an irresponsible manner. But he is one of the straightest and finest men I have known and if character counts as it does he counts for a great deal." All such views of Panditji become relevant when we try to analyse his attitude towards the Nepali revolutionaries. The happenings in Nepal drew Jai Prakash Narayan and Pandit Jawaharlal Nehru further apart.

PANDIT NEHRU's ATTITUDE TOWARDS NEPALESE POLITICS

With China consolidating its position in Tibet, Nepal came to acquire a sensitive and strategic importance. The King of Nepal for long a puppet in the hands of the Ranas, came to Delhi and sought political asylum. He was given a rousing welcome. Nehru took this as an opportunity to show to the world community his statesmanship and liberalism. S. Gopal narrates the story: "Now an occasion had arisen which could be utilized to strengthen India's position in Nepal, but clearly the cards would have to be played carefully. China was on the alert, while the British ambassador who exercised a powerful influence in Nepal, was in sympathy with the Ranas. "Nehru's policy was to compel the Ranas to carry out political reforms which would redeem autocracy and to receive the King back and to effect this by pressure rather than open support to Nepali Congress. It was not that Nehru disapproved of the Congress, but he did not wish to promote a messy and drawn out situation of fighting between popular elements and the Royal Nepal army. So, when Nepali Congress started a revolt and B.P. Koirala came to Delhi seeking military support, Nehru declined to see him but kept Koirala informed, to prevent a civil war and establishment of constitutional government. This kind of subtelty angered Jai Prakash Narayan. He wrote to Nehru: "So this is how you wish to treat a democratic revolution in a neighbouring state... you are destroying yourself. One by one you are denying your noble ideals. You are compromising, you are yielding. You are strangling your friends and slipping into the parlour of your enemies..."[3] To this charge Nehru replied: "I am distressed at the lack of understanding you have shown and I am more distressed by the astonishing stupidity, some of the things that the leaders of Nepali Congress are responsible for... I quite agree with you that the opportunity of securing freedom for Nepal has come and the trump cards are there. When I see this opportunity being almost lost and every kind of bungling being done by amateur politicians who know nothing about politics and less about insurrection, I have a right to be upset... Nothing can stop a revolution in Nepal except the folly of those who are supporting it... widespread propaganda is being carried on by our opponents abroad to show that this is just an example of Indian imperialism and that we have engineered all this. This obviously can do a great deal of harm to the whole movement. We cannot ignore external forces at work against us. What Koirala suggested would have put an end to the idea of an indigenous movement and make it just an adventure of Indian government. That is just what I am afraid of, adventurist tactics in politics or warfare seldom succeed. Daring does succeed and the risk may be taken but adventurism is infantile."[4]

Well, Pandit Jawaharlal, the Prime Minister of India could characterise the Nepali Congress leadership including BP (who had fought in India's freedom struggle for independence) as an amateur adventurist and get away with it.

There is no doubt that, in reinstating King Tribhuvan, Pandit Nehru had played a key role. In fact, Panditji informed the British Government that it might become almost impossible for him to attend Commonwealth Prime Ministers Conference in January 1951, if they recognised boy King whom Ranas had enthroned in the place of his grandfather. Pandit Nehru's tactics paid. Ranas lost their first battle. Ranas could not do anything without the support of the British and the British had to depend on Nehru for the success of Commonwealth. Later events show that Pandit Nehru succumbed to his role of being a mentor and behaved in a way that the revolution of Nepal was waylaid. Nepali Congress which had started a revolution, tamely settled down to a coalition government with the same Ranas against whom they had picked up arms. When asked why the coalition ministry broke down, BP had this to say, "As a party of revolution, we entered the coalition ministry to ensure that democracy really comes to the country. But there were various pulls and great tension. Firstly, the Ranas were very forceful, the King was there and Indian too pressing to become the peace maker. All these became too much for Nepali Congress to stand: so the coalition broke down."

It was not the first time that Panditji had played his role in Nepali politics. An interesting episode was narrated by K.P. Bhattarai, member of Pratinidhi Sabha, in June 1960 : "When I reached Delhi I found a telegram waiting for me saying all workers (Biratnagar) have been arrested. Then began the two Satayagrahas under Nepali Rastriya Congress. The first was withdrawn as Nehru personally asked us to do so. Both me and M.P. Koirala issued a statement, because of Nehru's advice we are withdrawing our movement. Our executive meeting was also held in Delhi. News reporters asked M.P. Koirala as to what Nehru had said, M.P. Koirala replied that Nehru had asked for withdrawal of the movement. The next day a long story came out in newspapers that Indian government was helping Nepali Rastriya Congress. When we reached Banaras, we found a message sent by Jai Prakash Narayan to immediately contradict the report as Nehru's position vis-a-vis the Ranas was most embarrassing. We at once sent our contradiction." Nehru suffered a kind of dilemma as far as Nepal was concerned. He writes, "We must treat Nepal as friendly country. Although we are anxious that there should be domestic reforms there.The country is backward and if it does not change soon enough, it is bound to face trouble. We have impressed this on authorities there. The position is peculiar as you no doubt know. Our policy is that we permit normal Constitutional agitation in India in regard to reforms and changes in Nepal. But we can't permit any attempt of violence or preparation for violence." India's position vis-a-vis Nepal was again made clear by Pandit Nehru at a press conference in 1954. "So far as Nepal is concerned, it is a well known fact, it is contained in our treaties and other agreements with Nepal that we have special position in Nepal, not interfering with their independence either."[5]

Pandit Nehru's reaction to the happenings in Nepal at that time was "we are functioning with strict neutrality, after two or three days of confusion on the Nepal border when it was difficult to know what was happening and proper orders could not be issued, we have made our position fairly clear and stated that we will not tolerate armed forces or bands entering India from Nepal or Nepal from India. Realising that a continuation of this conflict will be injurious both to Nepal and to India, we have suggested a ceasefire to the Nepalese government and peaceful discussion... indeed there has been a tendency on the part of the Nepal government to be somewhat discourteous to us and of course not to follow our advice. I don't know therefore, whether they will accept our suggestion or not. I feel sure that if they don't they will suffer for it. They rely perhaps on some kind of diplomatic assistance from some great powers."[9]

In the meanwhile, vested and reactionary elements managed to organise themselves and were constantly working for political instability in the country. BP was not satisfied by political turn of events taking shape in Nepal. Repeatedly he said, "Things were not ideal for a democratic set up". People had shown their disapproval of Indian interference. On the 10th May 1954, BP says, "It is a fact there is widespread feeling in Nepal against India and it is the later's policy of interference in Nepal's internal matters which is responsible for it." BP's only mission during those days seems to be centred on building a healthy trend, revolutionizing the basic fabric of the country, laying the foundation of a democratic set-up.

BP's REACTIONS TO INDIA's INTERFERENCE

In 1959, when tension with China was building up, Nehru declared in one breath "in case of an aggression India would defend Sikkim, Bhutan and Nepal". These utterances immediately led to uproars in Kathmandu. There were demonstrations, protests, meetings and agitations witnessed everywhere.

The sovereignty of Nepal was sacred to BP and he would not permit any one to take liberty to undermine it. At the time of Korla Pass incidence when Pandit Nehru offered help, B.P. Koirala in his statement to parliament said, "Nepal is a fully sovereign and independent nation. It decides its external and home policy according to its own judgement and its own liking, without ever referring to any outside authorities. Our treaty of peace and friendship with India affirms this. I take Mr. Nehru's statement as an expression of friendship that in case of aggression against Nepal, India would send help if such help was ever sought. It would never be taken as suggesting that India could take unilateral action."[6]

Pandit Nehru reacting quite normally said, "I was not aware even that I was making some novel statement and Mr. B.P. Koirala has correctly interpreted it." BP knew that "we have got to live with the countries south of the Himalayas in amiability and friendship. We may quarrel as brothers, in fact we do quarrel, but we have to live in the same house—this is our attitude. I am not afraid of what people say about my connections with India."

The reactionary elements seized this opportunity for denouncing the Nepali Congress and its leaders. BP says, "Every time that I come back after treatment from Europe, I face demonstrations by hired people. One of the slogans called me the running dog of Indian imperialism, but I don't think that has hurt my politics. My friendship with Indian leaders does not prevent me from being an ardent nationalist. I have been telling some of my detractors that Indian leaders should be aware of me rather me being aware of them." India's successful role in restoring the almost lost Kingdom to King Tribhuvan enabled Nehru to play in the subsequent years the twin role of a guardian and a reformer. Naturally, this led to many kinds of interferences in Nepal's day-to-day affairs. At times it was alleged that Indian officials those days even sat in the meetings of the cabinet and other high level bodies. Moreover, as the writings of that period indicate Indian officials working in Nepal carried a sense of superiority, which alienated a good section of politically conscious and educated Nepalese. In course of time such mistakes were corrected but the earlier impression still persists.

Beni Bahadur Karki, a leader of Gorkha Parishad, a party in opposition, said on 28th May, 1960. "During C.P.N. Singh's[8] Ambassadorship Indian interference reached a zenith. Everywhere Indians started interfering. The King's private secretary was Gobind Narain, an Indian. Cabinet meetings were regularly attended by Indian representatives. Anybody who wanted to take independent stand was thrown out of the cabinet. The military mission was the most hated. India has built Tribhuvan Rajpath which is utterly useless for business and commerce purpose. For that reason, we are going to have a shorter route. Tribhuvan Rajpath shows only India's strategic interest in Nepal and nothing else."

BP charged the Indian ambassador, C.P.N. Singh[9] for meddling too much in Nepal's internal affairs', to which C.P.N. Singh replied "we cannot remain completely dis-interested towards political and economic development in Nepal in the interest of our own security."

There is no doubt that in shaping the Nepal of today, India played a crucial role. The Indian independence brought a new era on the sub-continent. But the old British policy towards Nepal continued without any change. This is quite understandable for India having just gained her own independence. There was an enormous legacy of imperial treaties and agreements. It could not have been possible for free India to formulate a new set of policies in a short time. Besides, faced with pressing problems—partition, refugees and other issues—which needed immediate attention, Indian government at that time could not give better thought to the problems of Indo-Nepalese relations. Things were allowed to take their own course and settle down. This attitude was responsible for creating many kinds of confusions and misunderstanding. Immediately after the upheavals, the Indo-Nepalese treaty of 1950 was signed. This treaty in appearance was almost a copy of the treaty of 1923 which was signed between imperialist Britain and the Ranas. In fact, much of the irritation in the Nepalese mind was caused by this treaty. It was considered undignified on the part of free India to follow in the footsteps of her imperialist rulers. While giving his opinion about the Indo-Nepal treaty in 1979 B.P. said, "The treaty has weathered various terms and various types of governments, including spells of direct rule of king himself, and witnessed three major wars in which one of the contracting party was involved. You have yourself to judge how far the treaty has cramped Nepal's efforts to project herself as an independent sovereign country of the world. So far as my position in this regard is concerned I would like to refer to my statement on this question when I was the Prime Minister. Now, specifically you should have addressed this question if you were in existence then, to all the previous governments subsequent to 1950 treaty, pointedly to the king who has ruled directly, and to the present government when you are in fact very much in existence, rather than to me, who would only hopefully represent the successor government in the future. I make this suggestion to you hoping that you would get an authoritative answer to the question whether the sovereign character of the country is compromised and her role in the international field is affected by the existence of the treaty."

In 1950-52, India was in a position to give a more positive and perhaps less interfering lead to Nepal on a steadier path for democratic reforms. At that time India's prestige was high and for all practical purposes Nepal was dependent on India. A chance, however, was missed. In the end, India was neither able to win back the confidence of the people of Nepal nor serve the cause of democracy. India's confusion was fully exploited by the Monarch and his clique, while the revolutionaries who had sacrificed everything felt hurt and neglected by India. Later on, India on her part naturally felt cheated.

BP's DILEMMA

Pandit Jawaharlal Nehru had already dismissed Nepali Congress leader as, "young and inexperienced who had not shown any tact that is so necessary in a delicate situation." BP was in a dilemma while dealing with India. If he showed any leniency towards India, his conservative and communist opponents would join hands to topple his elected government. He so much wanted his friends in India to realize his delicate position. Perhaps it was too much, for there came about a kind of coolness in Nepal-India relation. In fact, at times, in the international arena, India had played a role to undermine the Nepali Congress. A very reluctant King made him the Prime Minister and an unwilling Pandit Jawaharlal Nehru had to accept him. But Pandit Jawaharlal Nehru's reaction to the coup of 1960 that "King's action has meant a reversal of democracy," came quiet unexpected to King Mahendra and pro-King factions. They had not thought that Nehru would defend BP so strongly. Official quarters went out of the way to project that King's proclamation in letter and spirit shows that democracy had not really suffered a set-back. Rather, the takeover was necessary to curb the growth of Communism in Nepal. Later, however this plea was never mentioned.

BP's socialist thinking perhaps did not appeal to Pandit Nehru, for he already had shown his reservations regarding the socialist leadership of that time. Otherwise, how could Pandit

Nehru be unaware of the only leader of Nepal who had an untarnished life of sacrifice and working tirelessly for the upliftment of the downtrodden? Nehru himself a true democrat and great parliamentarian could not but spontaneously denounce the coup as "a reversal of democracy". Kathmandu interpreted it as yet another instance of Indian interference in Nepal and used it to fan anti-India feeling to such an extent that the *Statesman* correspondent reported on the 5th January, 1961 that "the spate of anti-India and anti-Nehru propaganda that has been let loose had to be seen to be believed." In this hysteria, the King removed the democratically elected Prime Minister and his cabinet ministers in the four walls of prison. And Nepali people almost forgot the basic issue in this palace sponsored frenzy.

Sarvapalli Gopal writes, "When king Mahendra dismissed and arrested his ministers and proclaimed a dictatorship, Nehru made no secret of the fact that his political instinct has been outraged and decided that his government, while respecting the sovereignty of Nepal, would only carry on with the existing projects of assistance in that country and undertake no new ones."[12] But the fact speaks differently. During 1960-70, India raised the quantum of aid to Nepal two hundred and seventy times more than the volume spent during the previous decade, 1950-60. From 1963 onwards India first went out of its way to appease the King. Trade and Transit Treaty was signed and to Nepal was given the option to control unauthorised trade. Karnali hydro electric project, Panchmeshwar dam, bridge on river Narayani were completed. The Indian aid package to some extent helped to strengthen the hands of autocracy against the democratic forces in Nepal. Those were the bad days for the workers of Nepali Congress for they were being hounded by the King's stooges from all over the country. In the minds of common man in Nepal, India's prestige went rock bottom. India, from an earlier dictating position was now seeking co-operation and understanding from the King. A letter written by Nehru to King Mahendra appears to be pleading that ultimately it would be in Nepal's own interest since there is little in common between China and Nepal. "We feel that friendly relations with India would itself prevent any possible Chinese aggression." The objective of India's policy towards Nepal seems to have been ambiguous from the very beginning. The idealist approach of Prime Minister Jawaharlal Nehru to see Nepal moving towards a progressive democratic order got mixed up with highly utilitarian purpose to include Nepal as a vital partner in India's defence. These two considerations have alternated according to the variations in the situations. By and large, by this time border security seems to have become Pandit Nehru's primary concern. To tarnish the international image of Pandit Jawaharlal Nehru, China started providing all kinds of help to Nepal. King Mahendra displayed his skills of baiting one against the other on the Chinese factors. Gupta says, "In fact the basic weakness of B.P. Koirala's government despite the free and independent policies which it pursued in home and foreign affairs, had been that it was not considered sufficiently nationalist by elements both inside and outside the administration. Later, the aggravation of border dispute between India and China created more embarrassment to the elected government and a fear was generated that in moments of crisis it would fail to safegaurd Nepal's national interest. Thus the deterioration of Indo-China relation was one of the indirect causes of Koirala's downfall."[13] The dilemma which Nehru faced deserves sympathies. Due to Chinese aggressive designs, Indian government was feeling uneasy. Improved relations with her neighbours had become so very crucial for India. Once Nehru came to know that BP was keeping indifferent health in jail, without hesitating he wrote a personal letter to King Mahendra saying, "Koirala who is very ill should be given all medical facilities, and his own doctor, if necessary, should be allowed to attend on him." He in the same letter appealed to the King to take humanitarian approach to this problem. Neither the King's diapproval nor the country's requirements could deter Pandit Nehru from writing such a letter.

As to the stand taken by the Indian government, Bhola Chatterji says, "circumstantial evidence could at the same time suggest that New Delhi limited the volume of assistance to Nepali Congress to the concept of middle way. The guiding motivation of New Delhi was to have Nepalese politics restructured in a manner that would not thwart the eventual emergence of Nepal as a democratic polity." When many of the main actors have left the scene who is to decide whether this middle way taken by India was not a betrayal of the common Nepalese aspirations for democracy and socialist ideal.

REFERENCES

1. Nehru to chief ministers 15 August, 1949, *Jawaharlal Nehru: A Biography*, S. Gopal.
2. *Ibid.*, 1st July, 1948.
3. Jai Prakash Narayan to Pandit Jawaharlal Nehru, 17th November, 1950.
4. Pandit Jawaharlal Nehru to Jai Prakash Narayan, 20 Nov. 1950, *Jawaharlal Nehru: A Bibliography*, S. Gopal (Ed.)
5. *The Times of India*, 1959.
6. *Documents on Nepal's Relations with India and China 1949-66*, A.S. Bhasin, Academic Books Ltd. Delhi., p. 27.
7. *The Times of India*, 1959.
8. Anirudha Gupta in his writeup says, "Yet, notwithstanding all this, India would well be advised to leave the Nepalese totally unhampered to work out solutions to their own problems. But would that be possible? Non-interference in the affairs of smaller neighbours is an art we have never tried to learn." (Statement 8-9 Oct. 90).
9. C.P.N. Singh was vice-chancellor of Patna University, 1945. Ambassador to Nepal, 1959-62.
10. Rana Government had accused Indian government of inciting disturbance in Nepal by allowing the rebels to operate from India.
    Rana government had sought recognition of the boy King by Britain and USA.
11. Nehru's letter to chief ministers 17th Nov., 1950 letters to chief ministers 1947-1967, Volume-II, p. 229.
12. Nehru's note to foreign secretary, 5th January 1961, *Jawaharlal Nehru : A Biography*, p. 205.
13. Anirudha Gupta, *Politics in Nepal*, Allied Publishers Ltd. pp. 245, 249.

11

INTERNATIONAL OUTLOOK

Representing a small and economically backward country, sandwiched between two big Asian countries, when occasion arose BP demonstrated exemplary courage and took a stand never to waver under any pressure tactics. This shy, soft-spoken man could be a slicing critic when it came to that. To a man like BP who had staked his life for his commitments, theories of self-professed pandits appear irrelevant. While speaking to Theodore Jacquency he opens up, "It pains me to say that learned men in prestigious American universities write about soft states and hard states and authoritarian states and play with the ideas without understanding the ideological basis of dictatorship. Everywhere the revolutionaries with their back to the wall are fighting but never receive international understanding from these democracies. When democrats are shot down like dogs in the third world no voice of protests are raised. One after the other the potential democracies go under the heels of dictators and learned men in these democracies write books saying that this is the process of development. We democrats feel this way because we have staked our lives for these principles and we are abandoned." It is now well established that many champions of democracy behave entirely differently when it comes to the Third World countries. After the Royal takeover, the American circle of diplomats in Kathmandu with a great reluctance termed it as 'end of democracy'. The reaction of British government was that of relief because they thought it would be easier for them to deal directly with the palace in respect of recruitment of Gorkha soldiers for the British army. Prime Minister B.P. Koirala had been against uncontrolled recruitment of Gorkha soldiers for the British army. Developed countries were concerned primarily with their national interest quickly find justification for acts like that of the King Mahendra. Such are the pitfalls of democracy. The fact is they find it easier to deal with autocratic regimes than with democracies in the Third World countries.

NON-ALIGNED STAND

It was due to the personal efforts of BP that the first conference of Nepali Rastriya Congress held in January 1947 passed a resolution expressing solidarity with the people of Indonesia in their struggle against the Dutch colonial rule. Nepal similarly stood for Algerian independence. The world in the sixties was full of distrust. Many Third World countries remained non-aligned for the mere fact that they wanted to retain their independence to assess the political situation as it arose with unbiased mind. BP was very apprehensive about big power politics. Whenever he spoke during that time he made it clear: "One of the cardinal points of our foreign policy is our deep seated distrust of the political blocks and of regionalism. If we believe in a policy of non-alignment with any of the power blocks, it is because we do not desire to commit ourselves before hand to support one side or the other in any adventure it may choose to embark upon. We desire to retain our independence of judgement in the assessment of international issues as they arise. For too long, people of Asia had looked to west for justice. Now it was time that they took their own decisions. Peace in the world could come when there was dignity, freedom and security in the minds of a vast majority of common people."

BP IN THE UN

While addressing the 15th regular session of the United Nations General Assembly, B.P. Koirala said, "The drafters of the charter hoped that the great powers would continue to move ahead and strengthen the United Nations with sufficient measure of unanimity. But this hope has not always been realised and serious deadlocks have arisen between the contending power blocks on many international issues of peace and security. Under the impact of such new demands the function of the United Nations have undergone some transformation, and the role of the General Assembly has acquired a new dimension. As was proved by the part it played in resolving the crisis in Egypt and Lebanon. Nowhere is this fact more clearly evident than in the affairs of the Congo Republic, where United Nations has taken itself the responsibility of restoring order in an otherwise chaotic situation." He further said, "The foreign policy of Nepal is fully inspired by the principles and purposes of United Nations charter. We regard United Nations not only as a bulwark of our independence and security, but also as the protector of our rights and freedom. We look upon the United Nations as an instrument for promoting peace and justice among Nations. It is our firm conviction that an enduring peace and stable world order can only be achieved on the basis of freedom and justice. To this end we wish to cooperate with other nations within the framework of the United Nations. Within this structure Nepal had to play her part in the World arena." BP cherished a democratic, secular and just society in Nepal behind this international vision. He said, "We feel strongly that unless we develop economically, unless people are motivated, unless there are democratic institutions, our state cannot exist as an independent state. Sandwiched between two great powers of Asia both developing at fast rate we cannot just stagnate, vegetate, tuck away on the slopes of the Himalayas. We have got to develop, we must think in modern terms and we must think in democratic terms. I think this message must have been realised by the King, and by everybody in Nepal who has interest of the country at heart."

Reflecting on weak position of the Third World member countries, he says, "Nepal is fully conscious of her responsibility and the role she has to play in the deliberations of the United Nations as one of its member."

"Furthermore, in this Assembly, where each of us has a vote equal to that of a great power, our role and our responsibility have acquired a significance, unprecedented in human history. The great question now before us is how we shall fulfill that role. Are we going to be pulled in this direction or that, or are we going to stand on our own feet? Are we going to attach ourselves to one or another power bloc in an already deeply and dangerously divided world, or are we going to form our own judgement? Shall we be guided by expediency in an atmosphere of intrigues or by the true inspirations of our own people, our own reasoning and our own sense of justice?"

Time and again BP cautioned young members of the United Nations to be aware of the persuasive techniques adopted by the developed countries to keep their interests secured, they can be charming as well as stern in upholding their interests. In his humble but firm way, he said, "My country is fiercely proud of its independence which we have never really lost...while we welcome and we are grateful for the help that is being given to us by friendly governments of India, the United States, China, the USSR, the United Kingdom and others, as well as this World Organisation, we do not want any other country to tell us how we should think or how we should conduct our internal affairs." The big powers used foreign aid to bring the Third World countries to their side. Therefore, he argued, "We would be happier if the Aid which we receive were channelled very largely, if not entirely, through the United Nations, which has scrupulously refrained from any interference whatsoever in our domestic political concerns. Like other countries now represented, we prefer to estimate ourselves, the strength and weakness of other social systems and choose our own. We do not wish to be battered by propaganda or to have our minds made up for us or to reach our decisions in an atmosphere of suspicion and hatred. We do not want to be absorbed into cold war or become a tool of any power bloc. This is not only because, if a hot war should occur, we would prefer not to be embroiled in it. There is another and a deeper reason. We would like to join with other people who feel as we do, that the smaller nations who follow a truly independent course can become a force for peace in the world."

SELF-RELIANCE

King Mahendra placed a greater reliance on foreign aid. Even as a crown prince, Mahendra had observed in 1954, "From our friendly countries we have been receiving not only assurances for tangible assistance in resources for development of our country. It is we who should make good use of this assistance and co-operation".[1] While referring to his conversation with the King, BP said, "I told the late King Mahendra in a heated discussion with him in 1960—I think this was a little before the coup, perhaps in December itself—that the problems Nepal was facing needed total national efforts and if the King thought he could autocratically solve problems with foreign aids, he was grievously mistaken. The monarchy has been in power for nearly 20 years after that, and King finds no improvement economically, politically in any way. In our experience development in the context of Third World means, motivating people for the task of development, involving them at every level of development. So a socialist must concern himself with the development of democratic institutions. Foreign aid in our condition instead of helping the process of development only creates a new class of people whose affluence is unrelated to the economic conditions of the nation as a whole. This new class has no roots in the country. It exists solely on the basis of the manipulation of foreign aid and through corruption and illegal trade. Socialism is the natural outcome for the Third World and the non-aligned countries. Without an anchorage of socialism, the countries of the Third World would drift either to facist militarism or to dictatorial communism or to obscurantist reactionary religious fundamentalism. We socialist therefore face a big challenge in the Third World. The centre for gravity for socialism has shifted from Europe to the Third World, where socialism both as an inspirational ideal of life and as a model and blueprint for development has become relevant."

BP was accused of being biased against foreign powers and their aid-related influence. But BP says, "Even the king is worried on that score. As I see it, Nepal's situation can be symbolically expressed by a triangle, one point of the triangle is the king, another point is foreign powers and we constitute the third. If it were only a struggle between the king and us without having to calculate on the presence of foreign powers, this would have been a one-dimensional affair. In that case I could have told the king to hand over power to us."

In BP's view unless the people of Nepal backed by democratic institutions were motivated to contribute to the development process of the country, the gigantic task of nation building
could not be achieved. People's participation was essential. He
cautions his countrymen, "We must recognise outside help,
whether through UN or by other agency, however generous, it
is not by itself sufficient to achieve that goal we have set before
ourselves for the advancement and betterment of the nation.
The people of the help receiving countries must also actively
participate in the work and strive for national betterment.
People must realise that it is they who must work out their own
salvation." BP's scepticism regarding foreign aid has come out
to be true. When foreign money started flowing easily to Nepal,
a class of vested interests developed around it. They channelised
this aid money for their own betterment. Unless common
people keep a vigilant watch on the utilisation of aid through
political process Aid serves no useful national purpose. Contra-
dicting this King Mahendra always emphasised that "Nepal's
current problems are economic and those who raise political
slogans are ill-motivated."

NEPAL, INDIA AND CHINA

Regarding immediate neighbours, India and China, BP had a
clear understanding about the path Nepal had to follow. Sandwiched between the two big neighbours it was not always easy
for Nepal to maintain a non-partisan stand, especially after
1960, when India and China became hostile to each other. He
says, "We are too small a country to seek a balancing role. With
India, we will have close relations and with China friendly. We
belong to South Asia. We have a bigger stake in what happens
in our part of the world. China is our friend, yet, whatever has
happened there—say, the revolution that shook China after
Mao's death—did not affect us all as strongly as the state of
emergency in India or the (subsequent) transfer of power to
Janta Dal". He further elaborates, as mentioned earlier, "I must
be clearly understood that I am for Nepal, but at the same time
we shall have to maintain a friendly, most cordial and intimate
relations with India. One just cannot whisk away the fact of

geography. With all respect to the patriotic sentiments of a Nepali we cannot afford to be anti-India, we cannot take up the cause of those countries which are anti-India, pro-China or pro-America."

In his efforts to maintain a balanced relation with India and China, BP faced problems by the Communist groups. In his own words, "At present there are many hurdles being created by the Communists and ultra nationalist forces who are not serving the nation by creating obstacles in the smooth functioning of the democratic process in the country." G.P. Koirala, the present Prime Minister has however a different opinion. When asked about what constraints BP faced as the Prime Minister and what are his own constraints. Girja Prasad Koirala, said "BP had support of good comrades, he had a big majority and also in my opinion was not so irresponsible. Peoples' aspirations were limited, little things would make them happy. Nepal was cut off from the rest of the world. Whereas today Nepali Congress has a thin majority. This requires a lot of balancing role to perform. Peoples' aspirations have magnified. The world itself has become a small place. Nepal is opening up. This in itself is very good but the opposition should not make issues out of non-issues. Stability and democracy will have to be maintained at all costs."

BP's nationalism and pro-Indianism went well together. He said, "I am of the opinion that relationship between neighbours is governed by the mutuality of self-interests. If there are more points of contact or mutual interest with one neighbour than another, then necessarily there will be more treaties and agreements with the former than the latter." It is said, to counterbalance the alleged pro-India leniency of the BP ministry, the King, after takeover, had to give a swing towards China. The pro-China policy of King Mahendra in the beginning went off well but later three incidents reported in the government controlled press showed that 'balancing policy' did not always yield desirable results." Rishikesh Shah has summed up the prevailing situation of that time as follows, "Nepal's failure despite all out efforts to diversify her trade and aid sources over the last decade seems to have impressed upon King Mahendra's mind and the limits imposed on Nepali foreign policy by geopolitical and economic realities. "Indo-Nepal relationship, time and again have suffered from problems arising out of personal and political issues." Chandra Shekhar's, (Janta Dal President) criticism of the Nepali Government was stated to be India's interference in Nepalese affairs. These are the hazards of proximity.

As far as BP was concerned, way back in 1956, he had criticised Tanka Prasad Acharya for his policy towards China. BP maintained a balanced approach. In 1959, the leader of Gorkha Parishad, Bharat Shumsher, claimed that a Chinese survey team had entered Lipu area of north-western Nepal and had collected tax from local people. BP remained unmoved. Prime Minister Koirala had also said that his "Government was watching the developments in the Nepal-Tibet border area and there was no cause for 'alarm'."

It is true that, it was BP who first gave a call to the people of India saying, "They should strengthen democratic forces in Nepal, lest one fine morning they find China occupying Nepal by default." But later, he signed in Beijing boundary and economic agreements.

After the happenings in Afghanistan BP was afraid of Russian expansion. Sailendra Kumar Upadhyaya, pointedly told him, "you are obsessed about Russians why in this part of the world." He further said, "Russians have friendly terms with India. Do you think India will tolerate Russian adventure?" To this observation, BP's reply was, 'well' it is not the question of adventure, the thing is Russians are anti-monarchy."

The relations between nations should be based on the principle of Panchsheel. Other issues relating to nations should be solved in accordance with bilateral, multilateral and international arrangements and agreements with appropriate considerations. There is nothing which cannot be solved by mutual trust and consideration. That is the reason why BP says: "If Nepal achieves real national unity on the basis of 1) constitutional monarchy, 2) democratic political system, 3) growing economy serving not merely a tiny segment of the population but the people half of our work is accomplished. The task of acheiving national unity is solely, wholly and exclusively ours, and we should concentrate on it, rather than on others to do the job for us."

Regarding the role of super powers in encouraging dictatorial regimes, BP says, "They would be amused by my hostile attitude towards both United States and Soviet Union, because both seem to be interested in introducing communist authoritarian rule to the world. Russia does this positively and America negatively, by supporting unpopular dictators for whom the only alternatives are the communists." As Nepal's Prime Minister, BP had visited Iran in 1960. He told the Shah of Iran, "Monarchy should not be dictatorial it should be constitutional and, the people should be permitted to select the government of their own choices."

The Shah "...gave the usual explanation of dictators..." and advised BP, "You should not ride on a fast horse." When later BP's government was dismissed, he recollected Shah's advice and said humourously, "...I rode a fast horse for democracy because two or three months after meeting Shah, I was toppled."

REFERENCE

1. *Proclamations, Speeches and Messages of H.M. King Mahendra B. Shah Deva*, Vol I, July-Dec. 1960, Dept. Publicity HMG, Kathmandu, Nepal, 1967.

12

THE END OF BP—THE VISIONARY

BP's clarity of vision gets manifested when he emphatically says, "All this means that the people of Nepal have twofold responsibility—achievement of Democracy and defence of National integrity. If, however, we consider one of the two responsibilities as our only task, we would be one sided and commit grave blunder. And if we lay stress on the achievement of democracy alone, we may not effectively participate in resolving the national crisis. If we merely at that point pursuit of one sided task it may lead us into the snare of international conspiracy. Similarly if we consider nationalism as our only concern we would be led to slogan mongering for empty nationalism of the last sixteen years, and ultimately support authoritarianism. On the basis of this kind of hollow nationalism the inner strength of the people cannot be generated for the defence of nationalism. For these reasons we have to understand clearly that national unity can succeed only on the base of democracy, and the democratic base can take the country to the path of economic development and just economic order. We do therefore, consider that nationalism, democracy and economic development of the country are interdependent."[1]

Let us briefly look back at the people for whose emancipation from the tyranny of monarchy BP struggled throughout his life. The people of Nepal after the consolidation of their country by the efforts of Prithavinarayan Shah had seen many ups and downs. These were the people of divergent groups belonging to petty clans like Kiratas, Magar, Gurung, Khatris, Brahmins and Newars etc. There were many under-currents between the victorious Gurkhas and vanquished Newar community. The emotional integration between these divergent groups was brought about by one poor poet from Tanahu, Bhanubhakta. Jealousies and conflicts all got submerged in Bhanubhakta's ear catching lyrics. Such is the flow and beauty of his creation that even an illiterate Nepali could recite his verses without efforts. He was born in the year 1834. It was a time when Nepal was reeling under the defeat by the British which had led to the treaty of Sugauli in 1816. A healing touch was necessary. Bhanubhakta was there to provide it. His works once more inspired the people to believe that however intense was the immediate suffering, there always was an end to it lurking in the horizon. All sections of society found an image of their own self in his works and they embraced him as their own. Early in life Bhanubhakta had decided to translate *Ramayana* into Nepali. It is due to him that Rama had become the personification of every individual's ideal and aspiration. "In fact among the people of Nepal Rama is the most beloved and revered personality."[2] All his works, *Ramayana, Ramgeta, Badhusiksha, Prasnotari*, poems and short stories became immediately popular among the people.

The beginning of the twentieth century brought to Nepal a ferver for religious and social reforms "which threatened to impair the hegemony of the Brahmins and the priestly groups who also formed a section of land owning classes in Nepal."[3] People like Madhav Raj Joshi were forced to leave their home due to Rana atrocities. Joshi settled down permanently in Darjeeling. Books like *Makai Kheti Parva* and *Atal Bahadur Natak* started appearing in Nepal. Mohan Shumsher, Prime Minister of Nepal in 1950, could not perceive what his predecessor Chandra Shamsher had already noticed. Because of the changed atmosphere Chandra Shamsher even took initiative to open the first institution for higher education in Nepal, Tri Chandra College. Pandit Ram Mani Acharya Dixit reports an interesting incidence about this. At the opening of the college, "Naturally every Nepali was happy. I wanted to recite a poem on that occasion and sought the permission of Shri Chandra. The Maharaja said to me, look I don't know whether this will be a happy or a sad occasion for the rulers of Nepal. I can see it will not be a happy one, but I had to do it due to the changed atmosphere."

He further writes, "Even during the time of Chandra Shamsher, anti-Rana voices were being heard. *Gurkhali,* a paper had created a stir. There would be some anti-Rana voices coming from one corner or the other which were carefully suppressed by Shri Chandra. The measures of punishment were different for different people. Trying to be lenient towards Krishna Prasad Koirala but harsh towards the author of *Makai ko Kheti,* trying to impress the editors of *Gurkhali* through other channels were some of his routined works."[4]

Gurkhali published from Banaras for over eight years by Subba Devi Prasad Sapkota, gave much needed courage to the like-minded Nepalis to raise their voice against the authoritarian Rana rule. Due to Rana's insistence, this paper however was stopped in 1922 by the British Government of India. The Ranas took adequate measures within the valley to prevent any kind of organised movement. In spite of this, some young Nepalese succeeded in establishing a secret society called Prachanda Gurkha. Its goal was to end Rana rule and establish democracy. In the end, Rana police caught them and put them behind bars. Nepal's economic and political ills gave rise to another batch of revolutionaries who in 1935 established another secret society, named Prajaparisad. It is reported that King Tribhuvan was associated with this group. The aim of Prajaparisad was to end the Rana rule and establish democratic government under the leadership of the King. With some of his comrades, Tanka Prasad Acharya visited Burma and India in 1937-38 to learn terrorist activities. They planned to fight the Ranas on two fronts—by educating the people politically and by assassinating important Ranas—to bring about much needed reforms. Tanka Prasad managed to smuggle a printing machine which was kept buried in a pit. Kathmandu valley for the first time in 1937 saw hand bills littered at different places abusing the Ranas for their misconduct. In 1940, due to betrayal by the brother of Dharma Bhakta some five hundred people were arrested. The Rana police one day swooped down on its members capturing hundreds of them. After a brief trial its leaders—Dharma Bhakta, Dasarath Chandra, Gangalal and Sukra Raj Shastri— were sentenced to death. Tanka Prasad Acharya, Ramhari Sharma, Chuda Prasad, Ganesh Man Singh,

Hari Krishna, Govind Prasad Upadhyaya, Pushkar Nath and Bala Chandra were given life imprisonment with hard labour. King Tribhuvan was threatened by the Rana Prime Minister that he would be sent to Gorkha in case he misbehaved. The vigilance around the King and his palace was doubled by the Ranas. Few of its members however managed to flee to India. One of them was Ganesh Man Singh. These happenings confirmed people's perception that change had become imperative. When Mukti-Sena arrived, people of Nepal welcomed them. It was due to their efforts that King Tribhuvan got back his lost crown.

Over a hundred years ago Swami Vivekananda had said about Karma Yoga, "He works best who works without any motives, neither for money nor for fame nor for anything else, and when a man can do that, he will be Buddha. This man represents the highest ideal Karma Yoga." A compassionate BP was always trying to bring happiness in the life of an ordinary citizen of his country and was trying to follow in his own way Mahatma Buddha who had said, "Do good and be good and that will take you to freedom and whatever truth there is."

Once asked by Bhola Chatterji as to, "after BP Koirala who?" BP answers, "I am not modest when I say that I am not indispensable. Of late I have deliberately tried to keep myself out of day-to-day party politics. The responsibility of running the party has revolved on Krishna Prasad Bhattarai who is acting on my behalf, and Girja Prasad Koirala, General Secretary of the party." The second rank leadership of Nepali Congress is quite capable. A party which had suffered persecution for so long, a party kept out of power for so long has managed to survive. For the last thirty years when it had to undergo all kinds of affliction and hunt down yet has managed to come to power once again. This in itself proves that there is every reason to be optimistic about democracy taking deeper roots in Nepal.

BP had a clever mind and a straight approach. Once the correspondent of the *Mirror*, had asked him, "Where do you expect to get funds for your campaign in the context of Referendum, would the Socialist International be a potential or actual source?" Prompt came his reply, "From the people, perhaps from you too, we do not need any foreign source for our funds, however, open, frank and untainted."

During those decisive days he repeatedly said, "I have no new model for democracy in my mind. No new model for others to watch and initiate. I have dreams for my country one of them is to present to the world how a democracy is run." On the same issue, being asked by Associate Editor, Theodore Jacquency of the *World View*, "Many people believe that constitutional democracy for the Third World is irrelevant to development, a useless luxury. How do you respond?"

BP reacted vehemently, "Who is to decide who will be that authority, who will have dictatorial power to develop? Not Professors from Harward University. They are not going to select them. It will be some man riding on a white charger, who will say that I am destined to develop the country and the powers must belong to me. It is a very simple question. Even if we agree, for the sake of argument and I want to emphasize that I don't agree—that a poor country needs an authoritarian rule. Who will be that authority? Who is going to protect the people from that authoritarian power? Whoever has the longest sword? We will have to measure the length of that sword to decide who will have maximum power in the state. I react very strongly to this kind of propaganda. Unfortunately there are intellectuals who make these kind of arguments for the Third World. Ultimately basic question has to be asked : what is the objective of development? Is the objective only to improve the statistical number on a piece of paper or is it to make a man happy. If making people happy is the objective, then how can you make them happy by depriving them of their elementary human right? Russia has not made faster economic development under authoritarian rule than after the overthrow of Czarist regime. Even during Czars time the development was about as fast as it was during Stalin's time in Russia. West Germany has been developing faster than East Germany. I think that India has been developing faster than Pakistan, even though Pakistan has been receiving massive economic aid from outside. Moreover you cannot present this problem to poor people, this is insulting to the dignity of poor nations, to present the issue as a choice between poverty and democracy.

BP believed that Democratic Socialism was the only solution for mankind throughout the world. It was due to his efforts that Nepal came closer to International Socialist movement. He was representing Nepal at different world forums. Way back in 1952, he had founded the Asian Socialist Conference in Rangoon. His close association with Socialist International, Asian Socialist Conference and Asia Pacific Organization Congress, earned him a place in Socialist movement throughout the world. President and Chairman of Socialist International, and SPD of Germany, Mr. Willy Brandt said, "My colleague and friend BP Koirala, a staunch defender of rights of the people; of the independence of the nation; and just society, will be remembered forever, as an outstanding personality for sticking to his principle, throughout the world."

All his socialist comrades of those days remained committed to socialism all through their life in their own way. These brave men wanted to establish people's socialism rather than state socialism. Jai Prakash Narayan in his prophetic statement reveals to common man how they remained committed to their principles when he says, "The roots of morality lie in the endeavour of man to realise this unity of existence, or to put it differently to realise his self. For one who has experienced the unity, the practice of morality becomes as natural and effortless as drawing of breath. The socialists of yesterday who had high ideals tried to live up to it.

BP was a great believer of tradition, that is the reason why he said, "We have reached a point in Nepal's history when the King has to make up his mind whether he wants to save his throne or be an authoritarian ruler, kingship in Nepal has been a traditional institution the difference now is he has to like whatever is liked by the people. He should have no choice in the matter. He can't indulge in his personal likes and dislikes."

Talking to the Editor of *Vasudha*, he further explains, "We are firmly of the opinion that the national unity rests upon the firm foundation of democracy. The first condition of national unity is a relationship of trust and confidence between the institution of monarchy and the parliament elected by the people. Since the institution of monarchy is not subject to popular vote, it becomes vulnerable under political attacks and thus loses both its legitimacy, which is through conventions and myths derived from an unopposed supposition of universal loyalty of the people to the institution and its utility to the nation, unless it binds itself to work in harmony with the parliament. In democratic monarchy, the crown is an exalted institution within the frame-work of democracy."

Likewise a great champion of Human Rights, he says, "Human Rights bestowed recognition to human beings as a man. I have only propounded that man must live by exercising human rights that is why, basic democratic rights are considered as birth rights of a man."

As a Prime Minister while addressing a Planning Commission meeting he said, "There is a portrait of the King, it is a very appropriate thing. But there should be another picture—that of a farmer bending over his plough. Whenever you have a project or a scheme of development or a plan you have got to remeber that man with a plough and his hut. And you should ask yourself what benefits that man in the picture and not the King is going to derive out of your plans. It is not my original idea, it is Gandhi's idea". That was BP the man of the people.

On 21st July 1982, the announcement made by his brother Girja Prasad Koirala, from the balcony of his house, "Sandaju is no more, "brought spontaneous grief to the people of Nepal. The cortege procession to Arya Ghat was a scene to be witnessed. BP with his mischievous smile would have enjoyed the rendering by the sea of humanity with one voice : 'Koirala is immortal. We shall fulfill his dreams'. Sindoor, flowers and coins rained from all sides from the housetops all along the route of the funeral.

A chapter of struggle between three successive dictators, romantic charismatic leader and a true Socialist came to a close when BP passed away in his modest abode, in the midst of the mountains, among his people and the land he loved and cherished most.

REFERENCES

1. *Mirror*, July 20, 1979.
2. *Heros and the Builders of Nepal*, Shah Rishikesh, Oxford University Press, 1970, p. 91.
3. Anirudha Gupta, *Politics in Nepal*, p. 91.
4. *Purana Samjhana*, Sardar Pandit Ram Mani Acharya Dixit, Adarsh Chapakhana, Ramshah Path, Thapathali Kathmandu, Nepal, p. 155.

LIST OF EVENTS

1945	BP develops throat trouble in Hazaribagh jail
1945	BP starts his hunger strike (1st May)
1946	Dr. Duggan of Tata Research Institute pronounces throat cancer
1946	*Searchlight*, Patna publishes BP's letter
1946	BP meets Ganesh Man Singh and other revolutionaries
1947	Nepali Rastriya Congress established in Calcutta (31st October)
1947	First Labour strike in Biratnagar (4th March)
1947	Constitutional Reforms Commission set up
1948	BP jailed in Kathmandu - Gandhiji intervenes
1948	Contingent of Rastriya Congress under B.P. Koirala went to Nepal. Rana police rounded them up
1948	Nepal Praja Panchayat formed, October
1948	29 days' hunger strike by B.P. Koirala
1948	Padma Shamsher forced to resign
1949	Historic Hunger Strike by BP
1949	BP released from Rana prison
1950	Nepal sees Satyagraha for the first time
1950	Nepali Rastriya Congress merges with Nepal Prajatantrik Congress, April 27
1950	Baigania meeting decides to launch liberation struggle from within the country
1950	Armed struggle starts
1950	Pandit Jawaharlal Nehru announced Indian support to King Tribhuvan
1951	Tribhuvan returns to Kathmandu, 15 Feb.
1951	Democracy comes to Nepal, 18 Feb.
1951	Ten member coalition government formed
1951	Home Minister BP charges Gorkha Dal for anarchy
1951	Gorkha Dal banned
1951	Coalition government comes to an end
1952	BP presents his thesis to party men
1952	Agreement between B.P. and M.P. Koirala
1952	Indian experts group visits Nepal
1953	League of Democratic formed. Secret agreement reached by Nepali Congress. The Prajaparisad and Nepali Rastriya Congress
1955	M. Tribhuvan rests power to Crown Prince Mahendra
1956	Nepal signs agreement with China on status of Tibet
1956	Coronation of Crown Prince Mahendra
1956	Tanka Prasad forms Ministry
1956	Manifesto adopted at the Sixth National Congress
1957	National guidance council set up
1957	K.I. Singh forms his multi-party government
1959	B.P. participates as founder member of Asian Socialist Conference
1959	Convention of Nepali Congress
1959	First General Elections
1959	BP sworn as first elected Prime Minister

1959	Nehru refers to Nepal (Foreign Affairs debate)
1960	Presidential address by BP
1960	Sino-Nepal Border Demarcation Team visits China
1960	King Mahendra takes over
1960	Treaty of Friendship and Peace signed with China
1961	Suvarna Sumsher addresses people of Nepal
1961	Citizens Rights Bill passed
1961	Nepal divided into 14 zones and 75 districts
1962	Jai Prakash Narayan visits BP in jail
1963	New Panchayat Constitution introduced
1964	New Civil Code introduced
1966	Back to the village national campaign
1968	King Mahendra suffers a heart attack
1969	Kritinidhi Bist Prime Minister demands withdrawal of Indian Military Mission
1971	Revolutionaries from East Pakistan approach BP for arms
1972	King Birendra ascends the throne
1972	Nepali Congress volunteers attack sub-Police Station
1972	Legislation to prevent foreigners from working as agricultural labourers
1975	Dhankuta incidence
1975	BP's farewell to arms
1976	BP returns from exile
1977	Tribunal appointed to look into the cases of illegal activities of BP and his colleagues
1977	BP and Sushila leave for USA
1977	Proposal to make Nepal a peace zone
1978	Ganesh Man Singh freed from jail for treatment
1978	Pushpalal dies of heart attack in Delhi
1978	Administration orders BP not to leave Kathmandu
1979	Violence rocks Nepal
1979	Five member commission set up to look into students unrest and other incidence of violence in Nepal
1979	An act promulgated that elections to Panchayat should be on adult franchise basis
1980	National Referendum
1980	Grant of amnesty by the King
1981	General elections announced
1982	BP condemns rival groups in Panchayat system engaged in bitter struggle for power
1981	No confrontation no surrender to the Palace—BP's non-violence
1982	BP passes away

INDEX